Praise For Rational Relating:

In a world of fear, uncertainty, and conflict, Damon L. Jacobs focuses our attention on the essence of what makes our relationships - and our lives - rich and meaningful. "Rational Relating" is a must read for anyone who hungers for a step by step guide to finding or reclaiming passion in their lives. While other relationship books regurgitate the same old same old, Jacobs breaks new ground by offering his readers new insights into how we can maximize our relational joy.
-Dr. Paul Hokemeyer, PhD, Marriage and Family Therapist

In Rational Relating, Damon L. Jacobs expertly takes the reader though a process of redefining our relationships according to our own unique differences, rather than aiming for a "one size fits all" model of conformity. By learning to communicate more clearly with our partners and even ourselves, we are free and capable of creating the relationships in which we bring more of our authentic selves, rather than less. What a joy!
-Jacob Glass, author of *"Starve a Bully, Feed a Champion"*

Rational Relating

The Smart Way to Stay Sane in the
Crazy World of Love

DAMON L. JACOBS

Licensed Marriage And Family Therapist

BALBOA.
PRESS

A DIVISION OF HAY HOUSE

Balboa Press books may be ordered through booksellers or by contacting:

Balboa Press
A Division of Hay House
1663 Liberty Drive
Bloomington, IN 47403
www.balboapress.com
1-(877) 407-4847

Because of the dynamic nature of the Internet, any web addresses or links contained in
this book may have changed since publication and may no longer be valid. The views
expressed in this work are solely those of the author and do not necessarily reflect the
views of the publisher, and the publisher hereby disclaims any responsibility for them.

The author of this book does not dispense medical advice or prescribe the use of any
technique as a form of treatment for physical, emotional, or medical problems without the
advice of a physician, either directly or indirectly. The intent of the author is only to offer
information of a general nature to help you in your quest for emotional and spiritual well-
being. In the event you use any of the information in this book for yourself, which is your
constitutional right, the author and the publisher assume no responsibility for your actions.

Any people depicted in stock imagery provided by Thinkstock are models,
and such images are being used for illustrative purposes only.
Certain stock imagery © Thinkstock.

Printed in the United States of America.

ISBN: 978-1-4525-8177-4 (sc)
ISBN: 978-1-4525-8179-8 (hc)
ISBN: 978-1-4525-8178-1 (e)

Library of Congress Control Number: 2013916230

Balboa Press rev. date: 11/08/2013

Table of Contents

Foreword to "Rational Relating" by Damon L. Jacobs

Written by Dr Debbie Joffe Ellis

M ost human beings love 'love.'

    We may love family members, our friends, animals, nature, our work, art, theater … the list could go on and on.

It can feel wonderful and delicious to love. Many of us desire a singular connection with another person to whom we give primary focus, and that we be the one to whom they give such prime attention. For many budding relationships there can be a "honeymoon period", followed by a solid and healthy lifetime connection. For many others the "honeymoon period" unfortunately may be followed by conflict and strife in the relationship—particularly when unrealistic expectations rule the roost, and rigid demands dominate. The more psychologically healthy each individual within a relationship is—the healthier, more life-enhancing and lasting the relationship may potentially be.

My husband, Albert Ellis PhD, pioneered the cognitive psychology of the 20th and 21st centuries with his vigorous and empowering approach of Rational Emotive Behavior Therapy (REBT). Through his work he helped millions of people learn to love and accept themselves, and others, in lasting and unconditional ways.

The author of this book "Rational Relating", Damon L. Jacobs, is dedicated to helping others through his work with clients and through his writing. He cares about people, and hopes that individuals can enjoy themselves, and their relationships, and that they will make the effort required for creating relationships which fulfill potentials for greater happiness and minimal disharmony. In this book Damon largely draws on REBT and CBT principles, combined with his own ideas and clinical experience, to provide valuable information for those who will apply it.

He writes: "Rational Relating is about taking full responsibility for your choices. But it is also about honestly communicating your desires and preferences", and Damon shares the how-to's of doing so.

If having healthy and happy relationships is your goal—read this book, think about its suggestions, act on them, and enjoy the steady and sweet serenity which can follow!

-Dr. Debbie Joffe Ellis
-New York City, December, 2012

Introduction

S ara and Bradley enter my office bringing with them the looks of anger, resentment, and frustration that are so common in couples who are on the edge of their relationship cliff. They are in their late 20s, good looking, and well dressed in work attire. The only thing I know about them is that they have been married a little over a year and have told me they are having trouble with personal problems at home.

"Why don't you start?" he asks, with a tone that suggests this is more of a command than a request.

"I might as well," she says, rolling her eyes. "I am really upset right now. My baby sister is planning her wedding, the most important day of her life. And he refuses to go."

"Your family hates me," he asserts. "They treat me horribly, they don't want me there. Why should I put up with their abuse?"

"That's so dramatic. Isn't he dramatic?" A half turn to Bradley: "If they didn't want you there they wouldn't have invited you. He wants me go alone. By myself! A husband should go to a family wedding with his wife. That's how *normal* people do things."

Bradley sits up straight, glowering at Sara, who shrinks into a self-clutching defensive posture, still staring me for recognition of her suffering. "Oh, I should subject myself to your mother's insults? To your father's criticisms? To your sister making fun of me? They take everything you ever tell them about me, our private problems, and then they use it against me. You tell them personal things about our finances, about my problems at work, about our life in the bedroom—or lack thereof—and then they parade it out for everyone to laugh at during these family events. No way am I subjecting myself to that again."

"Fine." Sara huffs, folding her arms across her chest. "You just want me to be unhappy. I really don't know why I bother."

Bradley slumps back in his seat, having let off steam, and replies, "I don't know why you bother either. I work a job that I hate so I can give you the things you want. The job that your mother mocks is the same job that bought you that new car, that new kitchen, and that new nose. All I ask to be left alone and not to go to this friggin' wedding. Why can't you get that?"

"No, Bradley. Tell our therapist the truth. Tell him why you *really* want to be left alone."

Bradley opens his mouth, but Sara continues without pause. "Okay, I'll tell him if you won't." Triumphantly Sara turns to me: "Bradley wants to be alone to spend more time on Facebook with his old girlfriend. He thinks I don't know, but I've seen it. They chat back and forth all the time."

Exasperated, Bradley protests, "First of all, she was never my girlfriend. She wouldn't even go out with me back then. Second, I can't believe you invaded my private property and emails. All we're doing is talking. But Melissa listens to me, she actually respects me. And she understands that I don't want to be in uncomfortable situations with your loser family, and deal with the torture of being around them for any length of time."

Sara bursts into tears. "See what you make me do? How could you? What happened to the man I married?"

"That's another thing I gave you," Bradley exclaims. "You wanted that huge ceremony with flowing curtains and lace and flowers and all that crap I would have been happy going to City Hall with some friends and family and enjoying pizza and beers afterward. I sacrificed what I wanted for you and that means nothing to you at all."

Sara sits coldly. "So the solution is to punish me by finding the girl who got away and starting an online hook-up with her?"

"Maybe if you gave me a little attention and affection once in a while I wouldn't have to search somewhere else."

"And maybe if your penis wasn't so small I wouldn't be searching for it from somewhere else either!"

Stunned and confused, Bradley turns bright red. "That's great. Is that coming from you or something you told your sister?"

There is a moment of ominous silence. Bradley looks down at his feet and Sara stairs at a painting on the wall. She turns back to me and asks, "So do you think this marriage can be saved?"

"Without a doubt," I reply.

CHAPTER ONE

Welcome to Rational Relating

Relationships don't have to be *that* hard. Billions are walking around on this earth trying to connect with others and build meaningful and satisfying bonds. Yet for so many, there is something getting in the way of this experience. Something is often preventing individuals and couples from having the joyful life they want and deserve.

You would think it would be different by now. It's not as if this is a new challenge. Humans have been roaming the planet for hundreds of thousands of years and somehow we've made it this far. We have more ways than ever to stay connected: smart phones, e-mails, text messaging, IM chatting, social networks, access to travel. Go to any bookstore and you'll find dozens of books instructing people on how to find and keep fulfilling relationships. Turn on any daytime talk show and you'll see "experts" sharing how to have better communication, more sex, and happier unions. More and more American states and other countries are recognizing same sex marriages as valid and legally sanctified unions.

Given all this, why are so many relationships so unsatisfying? It is largely because most people are never taught the intelligent and practical tools of relating to each other rationally. They do not have role models or guides to demonstrate and teach the intricacies of negotiation and compromise. They do not understand that love, attention, respect, and honor must be given to oneself before they can be truly received from someone else.

And how would anyone know this? It's not as if this is ever taught in school. You are given training and skill-building for essentially every job out there. No one would expect you to be able to drive a car if you never learned how. No one would ever expect you to perform surgery if you didn't have the required education. No one would expect you to get into the kitchen and create a four-course meal without the proper preparation and instruction. Yet we expect people to get married and stay together for 50 years with absolutely no training or preparation for relationships. It's no wonder that more than half of marriages end in divorce.

Sara and Bradley's relationship is a vivid and accurate example of what can happen when two people enter into a union without adequate prior training and skill-building. They are both bright and intelligent people who have had access to Amazon's books, Oprah's insights, and more available information than at any other time in history. Yet neither has acquired the basic tools to communicate with a loved one, to act with integrity and consistency, to compromise and negotiate differences, to demonstrate compassion when hurt, or to take responsibility for their own feelings and emotions. The joyful life they want and deserve seems to be perplexing and unattainable.

This book offers a simple solution to that mystery. It is called Rational Relating, and it is based on an effective tool I have developed in my two decades of practice as a marriage and family therapist. "Rationality" is a perspective that prioritizes thought over feeling, belief over mood, action over reaction. It is a way of being present in the world and in your interactions with others that increases experiences of joy, productivity, and tranquility, while minimizing pain, stagnation, and drama. Rational thinking increases options, possibilities, and choices for one's decisions and behaviors. In short, it gives you more freedom than you ever imagined.

Rational thinking increases options, possibilities, and choices for one's decisions and behaviors.

However, implementing rationality in everyday life can mean you are going against the grain of what is expected of you in society. On a cultural level, we are seeing more *irrational* thinking than ever before. "Reality" television depicts and idealizes individuals who prefer to react emotionally and blame others for their moods and feelings, while actively creating problems and situations that lead to drama, which in turn, keeps them on TV. Social media is often used by people who wish to focus on a catastrophic problem, and/or express baseless arguments anonymously. Politically, Americans have spent the past decade shifting guilt from one party to the other, and one president to the other, which only adds to a limited-attention-span approach to negotiating complex differences.

It is long past time for a change. Whether we are talking about relationships with significant others, online acquaintances, family members, or someone in a "red state" or "blue state," we all can benefit from practicing more rational thinking, logical reactions, and compassionate practices.

Rational Relating is the first step in reclaiming a sense of empowerment, fulfillment, and self-efficacy in private and public relationships. It enables you to be mindful and focused in your connection with others. It empowers you to *act* in your relationships instead of *react*. It is the gateway to experiencing more fun, fulfillment, and freedom in all relationships by taking complete charge of your emotional journey.

This book will walk you through the step-by-step process of creating a joyful infrastructure that enhances connection and comfort in all relationships, including the one with yourself. It will guide you through a series of explanations, examples, and exercises that will demonstrate how you can incorporate more rational interactions with others. All that is required to learn this model is an open mind, a caring heart, and a willingness to connect with others.

What I Learned From Earthquakes

I began seeing couples as a marriage family therapist intern in California in 1996. To be honest, I dreaded them at first. It seemed that most people waited until the last minute to come to therapy to resolve their issues. So often I saw relationships dissipate under the pressure of frustrations and resentments that had been built up for years.

I always pondered this. People don't call the fire department after the house has become engulfed in flames. Why do they wait to see a therapist until the minute before the relationship is over? I aspired to find a way to help couples get help before the crisis that leads to the relationship 911 call.

Living in California lends itself to a certain degree of uncertainty and instability. The ground may literally shift beneath your feet at any given moment, putting a great deal of strain on building structures. I was living in the Bay Area during the destructive Loma Prieta earthquake in 1989, and saw firsthand what became of buildings that had a brick foundation with very limited range of flexibility or movement. Those were the first to collapse under pressure because they simply had no ability to withstand the trauma of the shifting ground below.

However, most of the newer buildings did withstand the shock. They were built to be able to endure and survive the stress of a major earthquake and its subsequent aftershocks. Many had damage, but because they could shift and move with the earth, they were better able to remain standing, as they still are today.

It occurred to me that relationships operate in very much the same way. The unions that are built on weak foundations, with limited or no ability to withstand stress and trauma, are the ones that collapse. Similarly, the bonds that are initially built on solid ground, with the flexibility to shift, change, and adjust, are the strongest and most resilient.

In the two decades that I have been studying and practicing couples therapy, I have begun to visualize every relationship as an individual structure, each with its own unique blueprint, complex layout, and intended purpose. And just like any building structure or home, every relationship has pillars that it depends on to remain solid and standing. If the pillars are strong, then the home is safe, secure, and less vulnerable to internal and external threats. But if the pillars are weakened, the structure itself is dangerously at risk of collapsing.

Just like any building structure or home, every relationship has pillars that it depends on to remain solid and standing.

In Rational Relating, there are five pillars that sustain and maintain the strength of a relationship in the long run. They are:

Integrity—Having your actions consistently match your stated values, instead of saying one thing and doing another.

Communication—Practicing the art and skill of effectively expressing your thoughts and feelings.

Compassion—Seeking to acknowledge and appreciate your partner, while minimizing possibilities of doing intentional harm.

Responsibility—Accepting that *you* are in charge of your primary thoughts, feelings, and sense of worth, not your partner.

Compromise—Process of releasing personal gain for the greater good of the relationship.

My job as a couple's therapist is to teach and assist in strengthening and reinforcing their relationship's pillars. By doing this, they can maintain a satisfying and fulfilling structure that is able to withstand stressors and traumas that can potentially weaken and "damage the unit" over time. I help couples learn how to survive the big and little "quakes" that threaten the emotional structure.

In this framework, couples are neither "healthy" nor "dysfunctional." They are neither "good" nor "bad." They simply have pillars, unique to the two people involved, that are strong, or pillars that need reinforcing. And like any reliable building, *all* pillars need reinforcing over time.

How To Get The Most Out Of This Book

This book is intended to be a resource, a companion, and a guide that will allow you and your partner to measure and increase the strength of your pillars together. Although you can read it in linear order, you may find yourself referring back to different sections at different times when your relationship needs "reinforcement" in various ways. To that end, I would not recommend you read it once and put it on the shelf, but that you consider it as a tool in your continued process of joyful growth and change.

I encourage you to learn these strategies, not only as a reader, but as a teacher. Consider ways that you are able to share ideas that could work for others who are struggling with their own relationship structures. The more you think about ways to discuss these ideas with others, the deeper the lessons will sink in for you.

Do not feel overwhelmed by the density of the material, or that you have to "get it all" the first time around. There are times you may want to set this book down and let certain concepts sink in before proceeding to the next chapter. Those are great times to discuss the ideas with a partner or a friend, and do your own journal writing about what you have read. If you get off track or confused about how the material you are reading fits into the metaphor of the relationship structure, then turn to page nine, which illustrates the fundamental House Plan and maps out the journey toward creating the most satisfying relationship for you.

Please be aware, all of the names and case studies have been altered to protect the privacy and confidentiality of my clients. Some of the vignettes are composites of the work with done with several couples, while others are examples of events that took place with a singular couple over a period of time. They are meant to illustrate key themes, not reflect transcribed case notes.

Finally, I am completely aware that some of the ideas and values presented may appear contrary to the ideas and values you hold. I am not here to tell anyone what to do, what to believe, what to think, or how to act. My hope is that the framework presented will enable you to create what is uniquely right for you. No two buildings are exactly alike, and no two relationship structures will be exactly alike either. But by reading this book and implementing the ideas, you will find ways to expand and increase the truth that is right for you, even if those ways don't fit for everyone else.

CHAPTER TWO

The House Plan

B efore we study the composition and construction of the five pillars themselves, we have some interesting prep work to do. This involves an exploratory look at our own attitudes and habits that were created and conditioned by the communities and societies in which we have lived.

There are five basic principles that are integral in creating a long-lasting structure. Or to put it another way, the following ideas are the "House Plans" that infuse Rational Relationships with power, strength, and durability. They are contrasted here as an alternative to the more traditional views of relationships taught in America, which are often fraught with pain, strife, and instability. As you read, think about which model feels like a better fit for you, and how you would prefer to connect with another person.

Rational Relationships seek to create vs. conform. In the traditional model of relationships, couples adapt their partnership and their family around society's ideas of "normal" without discussing, or even considering, whether or not these values are right for them. Decisions such as where to live, how to raise children, how to manage finances and where to go for vacations and holidays are made in order to conform with what people think they "should" do. The inevitable conflicts that stem from these unquestioned societal norms are frequently the very issues that lead couples to the therapy couch.

The problem with this model is that in an ever diversifying and rapidly changing world, there is no intrinsic "normal" or "should" that will apply to everyone. Long held traditions are being challenged and changed at an accelerated level, as technology allows us to learn about cultures and groups who live their lives and conduct their relationships in new ways. Individuals now grow up exposed to multiple ideas of how to dress, where to live, what to study, how to raise a child, and even how to express one's personal sexuality.

What one person in a relationship considers "normal" and "traditional" can vary completely from another's opinion. If one person leans toward conforming to traditional values, while the other person wishes to express more creativity, it can lead to conflict and resentment. We saw this in the opening example with Sara and Bradley when she insisted he "should" come with her to a family wedding even though he did not want to subject himself to abuse and ridicule.

There is no intrinsic "normal" or "should" that will apply to everyone

---

In Chapter Eight we will go into more depth about how couples can create values and practices that are meaningful and right for them through the art and skill of compromise. Suffice to say that if one or both members insist on rigid "shoulds" and make decisions based on the values of other people, it will promote conflict, strife, and a consistent weakening of the couple's pillars.

Rational Relationships act with consistency vs. confusion. How often do you get upset when your partner says one thing and does another? With small actions this can lead to annoyance and irritation. With larger behaviors, such as lying, deceiving, or having a relationship outside your agreements, it can lead to anger, betrayal, and violations of trust.

We often see the media present a sensational story that reveals a public person's actions as inconsistent with their stated values. It has become commonplace for elected officials and corporate CEOs to say one thing and do another. Political campaigns often show candidates drastically changing their policies and promises depending on the audience they are addressing. From mismanaging investments, to senators who vote against gay rights while carrying on same sex affairs, we live in a world that is facing a preponderance of public values and opinions that are out of alignment with private choices and decisions. How do you ever know what or whom to believe?

This same confusion and uncertainty can affect the way we relate to our partners and spouses. People may say they believe in values like monogamy, while having an affair outside their primary relationship. They may say they want to save money while secretly going on shopping binges. Or, they may say they want to preserve the relationship while doing everything in their power to sabotage it. We saw this with Sara when she appeared to be saying and doing everything to push Bradley away, all the while asking if this marriage can be saved. Repairing the damage caused by discrepancies between words and actions, and promoting consistency between stated values and behaviors, is fundamental in maintaining a satisfying and trustworthy alliance.

Rational Relationships express gratitude vs. grievances. As mentioned earlier, most of us have not been given adequate tools and skills to engage in rational, equitable, and loving communication with one another. Instead, we have been conditioned to use words and language to complain, control, attack, and demand. Most conversations I hear in local coffee shops, subways, or theaters, or read online, involve some level of complaint or focus on what someone else is doing "wrong." With Sara and Bradley, there is clearly a pattern of anger, disparagement, bitterness, and resentment that permeates their verbal interactions.

In Rational Relationships we start from the standpoint of gratitude and appreciation that the person sitting next to you is still sitting next to you. Before any problems are processed, I encourage couples to thank each other for at least five things. This sets a tone that is more loving, gentle, humbling, and kind.

We start from the standpoint of gratitude and appreciation that the person sitting next to you is still sitting next to you.

One of the hardest things for humans to do is to emotionally carry two truths, i.e., love and anger, together at the same time. Even the most rational of adults can be challenged to access a stance of gratitude in the midst of heightened irritation or disappointment. There might be times when you just can't "get there," and that's perfectly fine, as long as you are not reacting from an intensely emotional place. Over time, practicing gratitude and saying "thank you" enables you to breathe, slow down, and regain perspective. From there, you can use Rational Communication strategies discussed in Chapter Five to express preferences, desires, hopes, fears, and strategies for working through stressors in the relationship.

Rational Relationships focus on presence vs. distraction. I have often questioned why people still come to psychotherapy in the 21st Century. After all, we have the Internet and thousands of resources to transform our lives and manifest change. What exactly does counseling add?

In my opinion, therapy still works because the great Information Highway, and all of its resources, is no substitute for the presence and attention of a live human being who can listen, reflect, educate, and inspire. Similarly, in our relationships, there is no replacement for the physical, mental, and emotional presence of another person.

Unfortunately, we have drifted farther and farther away from providing this basic human connection with others. It is all too common for people to be physically present with one person while being mentally present with another. Texting, chatting, and social media have enabled us to have deep conversations with everyone in the world except the person sitting next to us. This is a problem that comes up in couples counseling quite frequently.

Compassionate intentions are a significant component to rational relating. This means giving your partner the gift of attention and presence when possible. It means you do not use words to knowingly and cruelly harm another person or denigrate their value. For Sara and Bradley, this means assigning quality time periods of being together without phones and computers. It also means changing the intentions of the words and actions they both utilize from harm to healing.

There is no replacement for the physical, mental, and emotional presence of another person.

More detail will be given in Chapter Six about the art and skill of demonstrating compassion in your day-to-day interactions. Willful and continued cruelty can do significant harm to pillars, sometimes even causing permanent damage. Using the framework in this book will allow couples to give and receive patience, kindness, presence, and gratitude.

Rational Relationships enhance connection vs. completion. Perhaps the worst thing to happen to relationships in the last hundred years was the construction of Hollywood's paradigm of "romance." According to these standards, a connection is made through dramatic circumstance, the couple overcomes great obstacles to strengthen their bond, the purpose of the relationship is to fill a void in the other (or to "complete" them), and then they ride into the sunset happily after ever. Such fairy tales serve only to tarnish and sabotage the real "romance" that is offered by Rational Relationships.

In an authentic rationally based partnership, each individual is already "complete" and "enough" prior to joining the other. Each person has worked on their own infrastructure at some point so they are not looking for someone else to "meet their needs." Both partners know that the function of an enlightened connection is to expand and enhance what is already inside one's self, as opposed to creating an illusion of wholeness and completion that is outside one's self. In practice, this is the most exciting and freeing type of "romance" that exists.

Chapter Seven will discuss the empowerment and strength that naturally follows from the acceptance of responsibility for one's own feelings and moods. Holding others accountable for our emotions can only lead to suffering, as Sara and Bradley demonstrated. They both showed a pattern of locating hurt feelings in the other, instead of considering that it could be their actions that caused pain and affliction. Through Rational Relating, they learned how to take back their power, and minimize accusations, blame, and pain.

In an authentic rationally based partnership, each individual is already "complete" and "enough" prior to joining the other.

If this appeals to you, then congratulations! You have found the right book. I encourage you to begin this exciting journey with an open mind , a warm heart, and a willingness to do the exercises that are set out. None of this is about perfection or achievement. The strengthening of pillars is an ongoing process. But, as you will see, the experience of reinforcing your relationship pillars can be joyful, affirming, and even fun! If you're ready to start on this journey, turn the page.

CHAPTER THREE

Laying The Foundation

Now that you understand the integral concepts involved in the House Plan of a Rational Relationship, you can begin the process of creating the "cement." Every adaptable and useful structure begins with the laying down of a solid foundation. Relationships similarly thrive when they are built on top of a strong base designed to hold up the "pillars" over time.

The ingredients of this cement foundation in Rational Relationships consist of three essential factors: rational thinking, inquiry, and friendship. I will go over each of these in more detail in this chapter, and why they are necessary components of an emotionally sturdy base.

Rational Thinking

Imagine you are shopping in a store on a strict budget. As you approach an outfit that would look and fit perfectly, you realize you are $50 over your budget. Your mind quickly processes two conflicting thoughts. "Come on, put it on credit, you deserve this."

Followed by, "No, I promised my partner I wouldn't overspend, I agreed to keep purchases within the agreed upon budget, I want to do the right thing." And one second later your mind returns to "Life is short, I can reduce spending next month, I'll look great at that party next week..."

And so on.

Imagine you are driving to work in the morning and you are running late. As you approach a busy intersection, you see the green light that is about to turn yellow. Your mind again considers options:

"Speed up, you can make it, it doesn't matter if it turns red, you can't be late today." Half a second later, *"Whoa, I may not make that light. And even if I do this is one of the intersections with cameras. I really can't afford a ticket right now. Not to mention I could hurt myself and others."* You will either conclude, *"Nope, just can't risk it right now,"* or *"Pray for the best, I'm going for it!"*

Sound familiar? These examples offer a glimpse into how the rational mind is constantly working, even when you are not fully conscious of it. By "rationality," I am referring to a set of beliefs that can be supported by factual evidence, reasonable conclusions, and cognitive logic. The examples above illustrate a chain of thoughts that takes place in response to a situation—wanting an outfit or a light turning yellow—that determine the course of action you will take.

You might not be fully aware of how much activity is happening in your mind. But it's happening whether you know it or not. Do you remember having to learn how to tie your shoes as a child? It was a process of trial and error that involved conscious thoughts in order to have a desired outcome. Now, when you put your shoes on, what happens? You just tie your shoes without the mental effort. But your brain hasn't stopped processing thoughts while you tie your shoes as an adult. It is still engaged in a process of rational thinking, decision making, and processing. Your brain is always operating, even when an activity is so routine that you don't have to think much about it.

The problems come when you use your unconscious thinking to tell yourself something that is irrational, distorted, or inaccurate. Just like you are not aware of every thought when you are tying a shoe, you are not always aware of the thoughts you are having when you are experiencing depression, anxiety, anger, or frustration.

The implicit theme of Rational Relating, as well as all forms of Cognitive Therapies, is that emotions, feelings, and moods are direct results of thoughts, beliefs, and perceptions. The idea is to start becoming aware of the thoughts that result in suffering, and then use a rational approach to reduce and eliminate painful emotions. Any time you are feeling something you don't want to feel, you can begin the process of changing it by asking yourself, "What am I thinking right now that is causing me to feel this way?"

You are not always aware of the thoughts you are having when you are experiencing depression, anxiety, anger, or frustration.

This concept was brought to modern psychology by the great Dr. Albert Ellis in the 1950s with his development of Rational Emotive Behavioral Therapy. However, this concept was not new to the 20th Century. Nearly 2000 years ago, the Greek philosopher Epictetus wrote, "Men are not disturbed by things, but by the view they take of them." Even during the 1800s Abraham Lincoln wrote, "Most folks are about as happy as they make up their minds to be."

So what are some examples of kinds of irrational thinking that prevent you from feeling content with yourself and with your partner? The following page lists a checklist of common thought distortions that result in suffering.

Common Errors in Thinking

When you are feeling depressed, anxious, or angry, you are typically thinking in a way that creates, reinforces, and sustains these feelings. Any time you are experiencing something you don't want to feel, write down your thoughts, and then check this list to see if they fit into one or more of these categories:

1. *All-or-nothing thinking:* You see things in black and white categories. If your performance falls short of perfect, you see yourself as a total failure. You perceive yourself, others, and situations as all good or all bad. Examples: If I make a mistake, I'm no good. If someone disappoints me, they are horrible. If a relationship ends, it means I am a failure.

2. *Overgeneralization:* You see a single negative event as a never ending pattern of defeat. You use one example to reflect on everyone else. Examples: That therapist was horrible, so all therapists are crazy. That movie was boring, so all movies must suck. That guy hurt my feelings, so all men are pigs.

3. ***Romanticizing the past:*** You focus on an ideal perception of something that subjectively happened in the past and use that to determine how bad the present is. Examples: Things were so much easier before. People cared more than they do now. It was easier to date in the old days.

4. ***Disqualifying the positive:*** You reject positive experiences by insisting they "don't count" for some reason or other. You maintain a negative belief that is contradicted by your everyday experiences. Examples: I did well at the job but that doesn't mean I'm a good worker. Lots of people have expressed interest in dating me but that doesn't mean I'm good looking. I go to work every day to make sure my kids have food on the table every night, but that doesn't mean I'm a good parent.

5. ***Catastrophizing:*** You make a negative assumption about something that will go horrendously wrong in the future without concrete evidence. Examples: I know I'm going to die alone if I get divorced. I'm sure if I ask him out he'll say no. I know this great relationship cannot last.

6. ***Martyrdom:*** You perceive others as not giving you the special treatment you deserve. You perceive all your good deeds and talents as unappreciated. Examples: Why can't people treat me like the important person I am? Why can't my partner remember every anniversary? Why can't anyone ever give me the respect I deserve? My partner should know exactly what I need when I walk in the door.

7. ***Emotional reasoning:*** You assume that your negative emotions necessarily reflect the way things really are: "I feel it, therefore it must be true." Examples: I feel my life is never going to get any better. I feel like I'm never going to succeed in a

relationship. I feel like I'll never get through this pain. I feel like she'll leave if she knew the real me.

8. ***Personalization:*** You see yourself as the cause of some negative external event for which, in fact, you were not primarily responsible. You take other people's attitudes and actions personally. Examples: You didn't kiss me when I walked in the door, are you breaking up with me? My partner didn't want to have sex with me last night, he must find me unattractive now. That guy didn't call me back for a second date, I must be a loser.

9. ***"Should" Statements:*** You carry rigid and inflexible beliefs about yourself, others, and the world, which frequently conflict with what is happening in reality. Examples: My partner should return my texts quickly. I should be making more money. You should want to marry me. That girl should have called me back by now. My mother-in-law should treat me better.

10. ***"I Need" Statements:*** You tell yourself you need someone or something outside yourself to make you whole and complete. Examples: I need to be in a relationship to feel valid and important. I need to have an important job to be content. I need to be thin to be loved. I need things to happen right now and not later.

★★★★★

Rational thinking enables you to increase experiences of joy, serenity, and freedom, regardless of the people around you, and the circumstances. By thinking clearly and logically, you are empowered to take responsibility, and open up to new levels of satisfaction. It also opens you up to complex and ultimately more gratifying levels of problem solving, which can significantly improve relationships with yourself and others.

"But what about feelings?" you may ask. "Feelings are not so rational."

I disagree. Feelings are in fact a logical and direct response to specific thoughts and beliefs. If I tell myself, "This book that I'm writing will never get published, it will never get read, and even if it does no one will like it," then I'm setting myself up to feel depressed, frustrated, and hopeless. If I tell myself, "I think this book will get published, it will be appreciated by those who read it. And hey, even if it no one reads it, my life will be good anyway," then I'm setting myself up to feel inspired, energetic, and at peace.

Either way, my feelings are a natural extension of what I tell myself. In the example above the former thoughts are irrational in that they employ "catastrophization"; that is, assuming the worst case scenario will happen and then emotionally reacting to it as if it had already taken place. The latter example is a more rational thought because it sticks to the facts and assumes a generally satisfying emotional outcome regardless of the circumstances.

Rational thinking enables you to increase experiences of joy, serenity, and freedom, regardless of the people around you, and the circumstances.

The biggest misunderstanding I have encountered while explaining these founding ideas of Rational Relating is that the concept seems "anti-feelings." For the record, rationality does not oppose feelings. Emotions and feelings can be quite wonderful and pleasurable experiences. They can be intensely sensational and fun.

The problem is when intense emotions are reacted to in a way that inflicts suffering on oneself and others. To put it another way, it is illegal to drive drunk for a reason. You may enjoy the feeling of intoxication but you don't want to be operating heavy machinery while your judgment is impaired. Heightened feelings work very much in the same way. Nothing wrong with them, you just don't want them factoring in when making major life decisions.

In the previous list, "emotional reasoning" is referred to as a tendency to believe that your emotions are factually true. Tragically, we have seen this happen all too often in the epidemic of gay/lesbian suicides in recent years in the United States. Dozens of young people have taken their own lives, and hundreds more have tried. The circumstances vary, but the thought pattern in all cases sadly went like this: "I feel so much pain. I feel so bad. I feel like I'm going to feel this way for the rest of my life so there is no point in living."

It is in a similarly intense emotional state that people strike out violently against a loved one. There can be many circumstances surrounding domestic violence, but certain ideas are fairly consistent: "I feel bad, hurting this other person will make me feel better"; "she should change"; "If I hit her she won't make me upset again." Again, these thoughts are not typically articulated or conscious, but this makes them no less potent and deadly.

That is why Rational Relating encourages a focus on calm, rational, and mindfully based interactions in relationships. Feelings can change all the time. Just like the weather patterns, moods are inherently unstable, temporary, and fleeting. You may feel passion, rage, euphoria, frustration, and elation, all within the same minute! If you react to any of these heightened emotions impulsively, you could do something to permanently damage someone and compromise the structure of your union.

Rational Relating does not take away from feelings. Instead, it enables one to experience more pleasurable and desirable emotions, while minimizing the suffering from painful and destructive moods. It offers a clear and practical way to enhance joy and satisfaction, while decreasing the cancerous bitterness, resentment, and anger that can interfere in the course of a gratifying relationship.

Throughout this book you will get a chance to see how rationality and clear thinking strengthen each and every pillar of the relationship structure, and how they enable couples to enhance joy and intimacy in their relationships. If this is a new concept to you, then please don't worry. It will make more sense as it is applied in each chapter. For now, rationality is simply intended to be explained as the "cement" and founding element in any long lasting and satisfying arrangement.

Inquiry

The process of inquiry in Rational Relating is defined as a quest for truth, information, or knowledge by questioning one's role and participation in any given dynamic.

Implicit in this description is the idea that you play an active part in all aspects of your relationships with others. When you are laughing and feeling great with a partner, you playing a role in creating that happy time. But when you are yelling at your partner on a phone in the middle of a busy street, you play a role in that outcome as well. Inquiry, then, enables you to look clearly at your part in every conflict, and how you actively participate in creating the outcome. Then inquiry helps you see how you can change the cause.

Typically what people tend to do when they are upset with someone else is to blame them for how they feel. *"He should have been on time." "She shouldn't criticize me." "He shouldn't feel that way." "She shouldn't argue so much."* The process of inquiry encourages you to ask, *"How did I show up for this?" "How did this person get the message this was acceptable behavior?" "What do I need to do to take care of myself now?" "What role did I play in the creation of this outcome?"*

Without inquiry by at least one partner in the relationship, it is impossible for long lasting change to occur. Albert Einstein once said, "The definition of insanity is doing the same thing over and over again and expecting different results." When both participants in a relationship find themselves having the same argument over and over again, it is usually because they are trying to resolve a problem repeatedly without insight, observation, or awareness. All it takes in this case is for one person to say or do something different.

Zoey and Andy found this to be the case during couple's therapy. Andy worked a job he despised, felt frustrated with his future, and started to feel life had passed him by. He responded to his increasing despair by wanting to be alone, withdrawing from social activities, and increasing his drinking. Zoey felt rejected by his actions, and responded by trying harder and harder to spend time with him and attempting to get him to talk about his feelings. The more she tried to get him to open up, the more pressure he felt, and the more he shut down. The more he shut down, the more anxious she felt, and this cycle created resentment and exasperation for both.

During one session, I began to explore with Zoey what she would do if she weren't expending time and energy trying to make Andy feel better. This led Zoey to share her interest in wanting to take a class to learn the self-defense system Krav Maga, which she felt she could not without Andy. Through inquiry, Zoey started to realize that she did not need Andy's participation in order to pursue new interests. Furthermore, she was able to realize how she was using Andy's "dark cloud" to keep herself from trying new things.

Once she examined her role in the relationship cycle of depression and anxiety, she affirmed that she was going to take responsibility for her own wellness, and started going to her gym for classes. Once the "pressure was off" of Andy, he began to explore his own participation in his depression, and began working on ways to improve his mood. As she became more empowered and strong, he started to learn that he too could take on new challenges and make some tough decisions about his career path. None of this would have been possible if they hadn't been willing to stop trying to change the other, and inquire within themselves individually about how to be a rationally and emotionally responsible adult.

Most of what we learn in our culture runs contrary to this way of thinking. We have typically been conditioned to think of learning as passive, thinking as receptive, and having our emotions determined by others. There are few facets of U.S. society that encourage and inspire proactive and curious inquiry into one's own role in how the world is running.

All it takes is for one person to say or do something different.

Inquiry starts from the perspective that you do have a powerful say in your world, locally and globally. You have an impact in your personal and professional relationships, your family, community, and in the world around you. If you don't like the effects of what you see, then change the causes, i.e., your thoughts and actions.

Inquiry is the literal foundation for you to take responsibility for your mental and emotional wellness. We'll discuss this point in more detail in Chapter Seven. For now, I simply ask you to consider inquiry as one of the fundamental ingredients of the cement that make the foundation of a Rational Relationship structure strong. When you start to change the focus of your complaints from the other person to yourself, you begin opening up new possibilities of serenity and stability.

Friendship

It never fails to astound me how frequently people choose to be in relationships with people they don't like. Why would someone voluntarily spend time with someone they can't stand? Well think about the home you grew up in, the kind of relationships you saw in your neighborhood and community. What were your family and cultural role models?

Clearly if you learned from your parents or primary caretakers that two people in a relationship are meant to argue, then you are likely to carry that idea into your own relationships as an adult. I have heard many people approach dating like an Olympic sport—a competition for who is better, who is smarter, who makes more money, who is more successful. There are rules, there is game playing, and you'd better believe there is a winner and a loser.

Once the relationship gets serious, the competition gets kicked up a notch. Conflict becomes the norm, arguing is the primary means of communication, and manipulation is the strategy for getting your "needs" met. These kinds of unions frequently employ "high stakes drama" such as screaming, yelling, name-calling, door slamming, dish breaking, or phone hanging-up as habitual forms of expression.

It never fails to astound me how frequently people choose to be in relationships with people they don't like.

There are several problems with this approach to joining with others. One major concern is that fighting can become a habit, excluding more rational and honorable ways to relate to each other. Getting angry over who is "right" can feel like a drug-fueled adrenaline high. Some people enjoy being upset for this reason, as it gives their relationship a sense of immediacy, passion, and purpose.

The other problem is that high stakes drama is hard to sustain, and often has to be escalated in order for each member to achieve the "high" they felt last time. This is frequently the point when I see violence enter into a relationship. Hitting rarely comes out of the blue. It is usually a natural outgrowth of the kind of aggressive and competitive patterns described above. This is not to say that it is ever excusable or acceptable to batter a partner, but it is important that we understand the irrational beliefs and aggressive communication styles that lead to violence being introduced into a relationship.

The good news is there is a much easier and more enjoyable way to relate to others. What if you had a relationship with someone that was based in friendship, compassion, and integrity? What if you and your significant other decided to stop blaming one another and focused instead on respecting differences, creating a solid union, and supporting each other's hopes and dreams? What if your partner was your best friend? These are the very goals of being in a Rational Relationship.

In many ways, having your primary partner as your best friend may seem counterintuitive. After all, isn't your best friend usually the one to whom you would confess your secrets, your fears, your guilty pleasures? Yes! And it can be that way with your current partner as well.

Think for a minute about the person you now consider to be your closest friend. What is it you like about that person? What do they give to you? What do you give to them? If they make a mistake, do you say, "You shouldn't have done that," or do you offer them compassion and support to help them out? Are you kinder to your friends than you are to your primary partner?

Here are some key questions to consider when creating a solid relationship foundation with another person:

- Do I like my partner?
- Do I choose to spend spare time with my partner?
- If I'm upset or sad do I want to turn to my partner for comfort?
- If something great happens, do I want to tell my partner?

- When I'm sick, do I want my partner to take care of me?
- Do I feel just as loving and concerned about my partner as I do my friends or my pets?
- Do I trust my partner?
- Am I able to accept my partner's point of view even when it is different from my own?
- Do I feel equal to my partner?
- Do I feel happy when I'm with my partner?

If you answered "no" to one or more of the questions above, then I encourage you to utilize the information and exercises in this book, including the explanations on rationality and inquiry, to think about how you can change the answer to "yes." Again, the goal of this book is to offer you guidelines and tools to be happy in your relationships. If you don't actually like the person you are with, it can be very difficult to experience the fun and enjoyment that you deserve.

Now that you have ingredients to create the "cement" of your emotionally fulfilling "home," we will proceed to the five pillars that will make your relationship sturdy, durable, flexible, and joyful. Once again, the framework is presented with the intention of offering you ongoing support and concrete information as your relationship evolves and flourishes.

CHAPTER FOUR

The Integrity Pillar

The first pillar of a Rational Relationship is integrity—that is, the consistency of one's actions with one's stated values and morals. It is the most essential pillar because it is also the cornerstone of the emotional structure. Without it, the other four pillars can easily be weakened and will ultimately crumble.

To explain integrity another way, you don't say you believe in monogamy and then screw everything that moves. You don't claim to want children and then refuse to reproduce with your partner. You don't tell your spouse you want to travel and see the world and then refuse to get off the couch. You don't state that your relationship is your priority and then consistently act in ways that sabotage it.

Sounds simple enough, right? But sadly, people find this pillar of the hardest to uphold. That is because it requires you to be completely up front about what you truly value instead of what you think you "should" prioritize.

That level of honesty, with one's self and others, can be a challenge. You were raised with morals and ideals from your family, friends, culture, society, religion, government, and many other sources. Based on the direct and indirect messages you received, you have developed ideas about how you want to live your life, and how you expect others to live theirs. When these values are healthy and flexible they are considered "preferences." But when they are rigid and inflexible, they tend to morph into judgmental "shoulds."

You don't say you believe in monogamy and then screw everything that moves.

My book, *"Absolutely Should-less: The Secret To Living The Stress-Free Life You Deserve,"* goes into great detail about the harmful consequences of implementing "shoulds" in personal and professional relationships. It offers a step-by-step framework for challenging and eliminating destructive beliefs in order to increase your potential to give and receive love, and live with integrity.

What if your own personal truth deviates from a societal "should?" For example, what if you are an elected official who has been told his entire life that homosexuality is a mortal sin against God, and yet you find yourself attracted to other men? If you have integrity, you will face the truth about your feelings and make political changes in alignment with your identity. If you don't have integrity, you'll either fight harder to repress your desires (which usually means supporting anti-gay/lesbian legislation) and/or you will indulge your urges in secretive ways. It seems like several times a year we learn of a senator who publicly stands opposed to gay/lesbian equal rights and then privately gets caught in a same sex liaison.

In my therapy office I am likely to see couples struggling with the problem of "cheating." In this context, "cheating" means someone violated their integrity outside of the agreements and negotiations of the relationship. Sadly, most couples don't actually have any explicit verbal agreements about acceptable or unacceptable sexual behaviors outside of the primary relationship. Some see cheating as purely sexual, some see it as emotional. These issues are rarely discussed before someone gets hurt. More often than not they "assume" the other is practicing monogamy without ever bothering to have an actual discussion about it. When I explore this issue they often respond, "I shouldn't have to consider that possibility in my relationship."

Without integrity there is no consistency in a relationship. Without consistency there is no trust. You have no way of knowing if your partner is going to say one thing today and do something completely different tomorrow. You have no security in believing that the person who seems to care for you now will still be there next week. It creates a state of confusion that often leads to resentment, anger, and betrayal.

So how is integrity developed and maintained in a healthy, loving relationship? It begins with both members taking time to explore, evaluate, and prioritize their core values and preferences. I begin by having individuals fill out the following checklist called "The Relationship Inventory of Values." They are encouraged to think carefully and honestly about their answers, and to circle the number that is authentically true versus what they think should be true. For example, if someone thinks she should spend spare time with her family, but in reality prefers not to, then she would be encouraged to honestly circle a "4" or "5", as opposed to a "1" or a "2" under the "Family" category. If someone thinks he should not have every minute of leisure time scheduled out, but in reality appreciates a structured planning of time, then he would circle a "4" or a "5" for "Schedule," as opposed to a "1" or a "2."

Without integrity there is no consistency in a relationship. Without consistency there is no trust.

Relationship Inventory Of Values

Instructions: The following is a list of different values that people may hold. For each value, please indicate how important it is to you, or how much you personally prioritize it. Please circle only one number for each value. If you hold values that are not on the list, there is a space to add them at the end. Circling #1 indicates very important, circling #5 indicates least importance.

Affection—to give and receive gentle attention and caring 1 2 3 4 5
Change—to have a life full of change and variety 1 2 3 4 5
Cleanliness—to maintain a clean and organized home 1 2 3 4 5
Communication—to effectively communicate with others 1 2 3 4 5
Community—to build support systems with others 1 2 3 4 5
Compassion—to feel and act on concern for others 1 2 3 4 5
Control—to maintain a sense of control over others 1 2 3 4 5
Contribution—to make a lasting contribution in the world 1 2 3 4 5
Cooperation—to work collaboratively with others 1 2 3 4 5
Creativity—to make my life unique and distinct 1 2 3 4 5
Excitement—to have a life of thrills and stimulation 1 2 3 4 5
Family—to spend extra time with family/relatives 1 2 3 4 5
Finances—to make and save money 1 2 3 4 5
Fitness—to be physically fit and strong 1 2 3 4 5

Flexibility—to adjust to new circumstances easily   1 2 3 4 5

Forgiveness—to be forgiving of others   1 2 3 4 5

Friendship—to nurture close, supportive friendships   1 2 3 4 5

Generosity—to give what I have to others   1 2 3 4 5

Gift Giving—to give and receive gifts on specific holidays 1 2 3 4 5

God's Will—to seek and obey the will of God

    (as I understand it)   1 2 3 4 5

Growth—to keep learning, changing, and evolving   1 2 3 4 5

Guests—to have my home open for friends/relatives   1 2 3 4 5

Health—to be physically and mentally healthy   1 2 3 4 5

Honesty—to be honest and truthful with others   1 2 3 4 5

Humor—to see the humor in myself and the world   1 2 3 4 5

Inner Peace—to experience personal peace   1 2 3 4 5

Inquiry—to explore my role in problems/conflicts   1 2 3 4 5

Integrity—to have my actions match my words   1 2 3 4 5

Justice—to promote fair and equal treatment for all   1 2 3 4 5

Loving—to give and receive love   1 2 3 4 5

Meals—to share eating and meals with partner   1 2 3 4 5

Mindfulness—to act with consciousness and awareness   1 2 3 4 5

Moderation—to avoid excesses and find middle ground   1 2 3 4 5

Monogamy—to have only one close sexual/emotional

    partner   1 2 3 4 5

Neighborhood—to take part in actions/events where I live 1 2 3 4 5

Nonconformity—to question and challenge authority

    and norms   1 2 3 4 5

Nurturance—to take care of and nurture others   1 2 3 4 5

Nutrition—to maintain a healthy diet   1 2 3 4 5

Openness—to be open to new ideas, experiences, options 1 2 3 4 5

Order—to have a life that is well organized and ordered 1 2 3 4 5

Parenting—to have an active role in raising a child   1 2 3 4 5

Patience—to be able to wait for a desired outcome   1 2 3 4 5

Politics—to be politically active and involved   1 2 3 4 5

Polyamory—to have intimate connections with

    different people   1 2 3 4 5

Presence—to keep focus on the here and now   1 2 3 4 5

Privacy—that mine and my partner's privacy is respected   1 2 3 4 5

Purpose—to have meaning and direction in my life   1 2 3 4 5

Quality Time—to spend focused time with loved ones   1 2 3 4 5

Rationality—to be guided by reason and logic   1 2 3 4 5

Religion—to have a meaningful religious practice   1 2 3 4 5

Responsibility—to acknowledge my role in

    relationships/events   1 2 3 4 5

Romance—to spend focused time with partner/spouse   1 2 3 4 5

Schedule—to plan events, even on weekends/vacations   1 2 3 4 5

Self-Esteem—to feel good about myself   1 2 3 4 5

Sexuality—to have an active and satisfying sex life   1 2 3 4 5

Sleeping Together—to prefer sleeping in the same bed   1 2 3 4 5

Sobriety—to keep my mind/thoughts drug free   1 2 3 4 5

Sociability—to spend spare time around others   1 2 3 4 5

Solitude—to have time and space apart from others   1 2 3 4 5

Spirituality—to have a connection to a higher Source   1 2 3 4 5

Stability—to have a life that stays fairly consistent   1 2 3 4 5

Tolerance—to accept and respect those different from me   1 2 3 4 5

Tradition—to follow established patterns   1 2 3 4 5

Trustworthy—to act in a way that inspires trust from others 1 2 3 4 5

Work—to maintain a satisfying job/career   1 2 3 4 5

**If there are other values important to you that are not listed above,

    write them in below and rate them:

_____   1 2 3 4 5

_____   1 2 3 4 5

_____   1 2 3 4 5

_____   1 2 3 4 5

_____   1 2 3 4 5

Now list below the 10 values that you would say are of greatest importance in defining who you are, that are your most central guiding values. Look back over the values you have rated most highly (at 1 or 2) and from those, choose your top 10 (in no particular order)******

_____

_____

_____

_____

_____

_____

_____

_____

_____

_____

Finally, rearrange those ten values in order of importance to you, starting with the single most important guiding value in your life, (#1), then your second most important value, (#2), and so on down to #10.

#1 _____

#2 _____

#3 _____

#4 _____

#5 _____

#6 _____

#7 _____

#8 _____

#9 _____

#10 _____

Once the checklist has been completed, and the values have been prioritized, I have couples share their Top 10 list in session with me. They are instructed to remain as nonjudgmental as possible, as criticisms and judgments may inhibit the ability for each to be completely honest about his or her values and priorities. Each listens to the other state their most important values, ask questions if clarification is needed, and share responses.

This exercise was the saving grace for Alex and Lisa's marriage. This couple came to me after being married for seven years, separated two months, and on the verge of divorce. Alex's biggest problem was that Lisa had recently joined a local religious organization, and he was steadfastly opposed to religion in any part of his life. She was frequently choosing to participate in religious and social activities at the church, which resulted in Alex feeling threatened, insecure, and believing "soon she won't have any time for me at all." With these feelings and beliefs, he gave her an ultimatum: Stay with the church or stay with me. She chose the church.

In our first few sessions, Alex and Lisa clearly stated they loved each other, that was not the problem. She felt judged and condemned for engaging in activities that were meaningful and fulfilling in her life. He felt lonely and scared for what this would mean for their future. He thought she was trying to change him and force him to have the same religious beliefs she held, despite her repeated insistence that he did not have to share her beliefs. Then I had them take home the Rational Inventory of Values.

Lisa ranked Loving, Religion, Purpose, and Community as her top values. Alex proudly listed Rationality, Nonconformity, Loving, and Humor as his top values. Both members believed that their actions reflected their values, and that they were engaging with each other with strong integrity. However, I noticed some discrepancies in Alex's list.

Although Alex claimed to value "Rationality," his reactions to Lisa were in direct opposition with that principle. He consistently demonstrated "catastrophizing" thinking patterns with Lisa, i.e., assuming that she was going to leave him for the church, and acting as if that was already true. The rational reality was that Lisa never wanted to leave Alex, and only did so after he gave her an ultimatum. I asked Alex, "Is it rational to divorce someone you love over a horrible possibility you invented that has no evidence whatsoever in reality?" Alex conceded he was being irrational, and out of alignment with his integrity.

"Is it rational to divorce someone you love over a horrible possibility you invented that has no evidence whatsoever in reality?"

As a self-identified agnostic, Alex believed that people had the choice to live outside the realm of oppressive religious structures. Yet he threatened Lisa with a divorce when her religious beliefs began to conflict with his own. I asked Alex, "Does a true nonconformist insist that others conform to his beliefs?" Again, Alex realized that his decisions had been in total conflict with his stated values, and realized that if he truly prioritized nonconformity, that meant other people had the right to choose an expression and practice that did not conform to his own.

With these contradictions illuminated, Alex made drastic changes. He began to realize that Lisa's participation in church activities was not leading to divorce, it was his acting outside of his integrity that was leading to divorce. He made a complete shift in his reactions after that, and agreed not to stand in the way of Lisa's participation. Although he maintained that religion was not for him, he was no longer threatened or afraid of Lisa's involvement.

This gave Lisa the opportunity to forgive Alex, move back in, and restart their relationship on a firmer foundation of rationality and integrity. In turn, she was willing to compromise aspects of her involvement and time in church activities, and at times chose to be with Alex instead of attending a religious function. But now she knew it was her choice, and she found she could trust in Alex's support because he was choosing to live in integrity.

The Relationship Inventory of Values made the repair in Alex and Lisa's relationship possible. It showcased each person's authentic values, and then allowed each to see how their choices reflected those values. But remember, this exercise only works if each person is willing and able to be completely honest about their value system without "shoulds" and without shame.

The Myth Of Cheating

Let's face certain facts. The average life expectancy in the United States at the time of this writing is about 79 years. That is predicted to increase given advancements in medicine and prevention of diseases.

Now let's think about a couple in their mid-20s planning their wedding. They are getting ready to commit to one another presumably for the rest of their lives. They are intending to share their emotional, mental, physical, and sexual lives together for what could easily be another 50 years. And you are going to tell me that neither one is ever going to experience a sexual or emotional attraction to another person? Is it realistic to vow to never have any kind of feelings or desires for anyone else for the next 50 years and beyond?

There are fewer injustices more damaging to relationships than the language of "cheating." Note, I am not stating that the act of "cheating" is what inevitably leads to divorce. I am stating that the way we *think* about cheating is what exacerbates pain, resentments, and ultimately angry breakups.

There is no such thing as "neutral" language. Other experts who write books and appear on television use biases in their language to describe a world of "cheaters" as evil perpetrators who hurt their victims. The use of the word "victim" creates a dichotomy in which one person in a relationship is actively "bad," and the other is passively "good." It is a reductive all-or-nothing approach to relationships that results in more pain and strife than the violation itself.

Here is the truth: there is no cheating. There is no "bad guy." There is no "victim."

What *does* cause upset is when someone violates his or her integrity. If Bob says he values monogamy while actively pursuing sexual liaisons with other people, then he is acting outside of his integrity, and that is the problem. It doesn't mean he's the worst pig in the world, and it doesn't make his partner a saint. It simply means he violated the integrity pillar; it has no greater meaning than that.

Will it hurt to learn of Bob's behavior? Of course! Will the pain and betrayal feel genuine when his spouse learns he acted outside of his integrity? Most definitely! But when you perceive his action as a violation of the integrity pillar, as opposed to something that was done to his wife, it removes the deeper blame and subjective meaning that many relationship experts wish to assign. Or to put it another way:

Basic fact: Bob had sex outside of marriage.

Reductive thinking: He did something horribly unforgivable to his wife.

Rational Relating Model: He acted outside of his integrity. It's nothing he did *to* his wife.

You might think, "How can Bob's wife not feel victimized by this betrayal?" Most likely, she will feel this way. But if she chooses to use Rational thinking, she will ease her pain and hurt by changing her perception of Bob's behavior. Bob's lack of integrity *affects* her but was not done *to* her. Once she makes that shift in thinking she is empowered to go forward, with or without Bob, with her own integrity intact.

"So anyone can do whatever they want and it doesn't matter?" Absolutely not. Rational Relating is about using the pillars to communicate effectively, and have discussions with your partner about monogamy that enable more compassion and compromise. More importantly, this model promotes *integrity* in one's actions, so that they are even more responsible and accountable for their choices than in the "victim versus perpetrator" paradigm.

When I work with couples who report "cheating," the first thing I want to know is what agreements had been made about sexual expression outside of the primary partnership. In most cases, couples do not have any discussions about this because they assume that the other person is going to be monogamous all the days of their lives. And in many cases, they are wrong.

Of course, having open and compassionate discussions about monogamy is much easier before someone violates their integrity than after. That is why I encourage all couples to discuss this issue *prior* to something going horribly wrong. It is much easier to prevent emotional damage than to repair it.

In these conversations, I help people get as specific as possible. I can ask one hundred people what constitutes "monogamy" and get one hundred different answers. So it is very important to be clear and detailed about the definition of "sex." Does Facebook count? Does Twitter? "Sexting"? Watching porn? Kissing with clothes on? The answers are actively created within the Rational Relationship with integrity, compassion, responsibility and compromise.

It saddens me to see how many couples break up and divorce because of an act that often means so little. By using a little more rationality, people can find an easier way to navigate these painful transgressions in integrity.

Instead of imposing rigid, inflexible, and unrealistic standards that set relationships up for failure, let's get Rational. I work with couples to create conversations about what happens *when* there are urgings for another, not *if*. I help people take preventive measures to maintain their building structures by having rational and compassionate discussions and compromises about monogamy. I facilitate opportunities for members to share their values, fears, hopes, jealousies, and insecurities in a respectful and compassionate setting. Sometimes these sessions can be very uncomfortable and scary for the participants. But the more they are willing to be honest with integrity now, the less they will need me (or a divorce lawyer) in the future.

Biggest Obstacle to Integrity: Shame

Each of the five pillars described in this book has a primary roadblock, or something that gets in the way of implementing change. When it comes to integrity, and completing the

Relationship Inventory of Values list authentically, the largest impediment is shame.

The word "shame" in this context means feeling bad or guilty about what you honestly want. For example, if I am a person who experiences sexual and/or emotional feelings for others outside of my primary relationship, I may automatically tell myself, "Those feelings are wrong. Those feelings are bad. You shouldn't have desires for another person. Your partner should be everything to you." With those thoughts, I will feel shame, and that will make it nearly impossible to complete the Rational Inventory of Values list honestly and openly.

Problem is, those feelings are not going to go away. They may be channeled into productive activities like work, exercises, or creative projects. They may be submerged into destructive activities like drug and alcohol use. But either way, those feelings and urges aren't going anywhere, they are simply being buried further and further below the surface.

What if everyone could simply be honest about their feelings and urges without shame? What if you could authentically share desires, hopes, fears, and fantasies with your primary partner? You can! But it does require you to honestly evaluate your true values and priorities, and minimize shame. Once you can admit your feelings to yourself, you will be able to share them with another, and build a solid connection that is maintained through integrity.

Fear of rejection is the most common response I get at this point. What if you are completely honest about your desires on the Relationship Inventory list? Let's say you made yourself vulnerable to a partner or spouse by sharing your top 10 values. From Polyamory to Parenting, from Cleanliness to Politics, if you clearly articulated your preferences, how would your significant other react?

The truth is, you can't predict for sure how someone will think and feel when you share this part of yourself. I can, however, affirm that living in integrity is the healthiest thing for yourself and everyone else in the long run. If you have chosen a primary partner who is freaked out, scared, or angry about your priorities, then this may not have been the right match for you in the first place. As hard as it might be, it's better to learn sooner than later if you and your partner have incompatible values. If, however, you have chosen to build a connection with someone who is rational, loving, open, and creative, then he/she will welcome the opportunity to learn more about you, and will look forward to revealing parts of themselves through this exercise as well.

As hard as it might be, it's better to learn sooner than later if you and your partner have incompatible values.

How do you get your partner to be more rational and open-minded? Ideally, in a Rational Relationship, there is a priority on creating versus conforming, as discussed earlier. This means that both individuals are invested in exploring new ways of connecting, instead of adhering to rigid and inflexible standards from the past. If you're not in a relationship where that is the case, then you may wish to consider getting some outside consultation, as Alex and Lisa did in the previous example. Ultimately, you can not control what other people think and feel, but you can *affect* their choices by demonstrating openness and rationality in your own life, and limiting the hold that shame has in your life. In the previous example, Lisa could not control Alex's rigid thinking, but she could demonstrate how to be open-minded and respectful of his values. Her proceeding with understanding, and acting consistently with integrity, increased the possibility for him to do the same.

If there was one thing I could give to every couple out there, it would be a magic wand to rid their world of shame. Many respond to this by saying, "That would be crazy, that would be madness, people would do whatever they want whenever they want."

I disagree. Rational Relating has four other pillars that promote consideration, agreement, and cooperation with others. As we will see, these four pillars serve to balance and prevent the hedonistic anarchy that so many fear would result in the absence of shame.

To learn more tools for living with less shame and more integrity, I encourage you to read *"Absolutely Should-less,"* and/or work with a counselor or therapist trained in the ability to examine and challenge internalized conflicts. Unfortunately, the practice of psychology in the United States has a nasty habit of perpetuating harmful "shoulds" and destructive ideas of "normal." Not every therapist is trained or equipped to help clients strengthen their personal sense of integrity and authenticity. It is always a good idea to first learn a therapist's philosophical and theoretical orientation, and choose to work with someone who seems to match your own ideas closely.

You can not control what other people think and feel, but you can *affect* their choices by demonstrating openness and rationality in your own life

---

Sara and Bradley On Integrity

I began my work with Sara and Bradley by having them do the Relationship Inventory of Values checklist as homework. They came back the following week reporting they had both done the exercise and felt both had completed the list honestly. I looked at each of their lists and compared their answers:

Bradley's Top Relationship Values		Sara's Top Relationship Values
#1	Self-Esteem	Affection
#2	Loving	Family
#3	Tolerance	Loving
#4	Gift-giving	Romance
#5	Affection	Sociability
#6	Solitude	Responsibility
#7	Compassion	Monogamy
#8	Quality Time	Compassion
#9	Sexuality	Finances
#10	Control	Community

Once I was able to understand more about each member's priorities, I had a better idea of how to work with this couple, and how to restore their relationship pillars. Then I was able to have the following conversation:

DAMON (D): Sara, let's look at your list first. I see you put affection at the top of all your values.

SARA (S): Yes, of everything on that list that seemed to be the one of most important for me.

D: What's especially interesting is that Bradley has the same value listed on his top five. Do either of you experience the other as being affectionate these days?

S: No.

BRADLEY (B): Definitely not.

D: Now Bradley, I also notice that gift giving is very high on your list, even higher than affection.

B: It is. It's up there ahead of finances; it's up there ahead of work. I want to be able to give Sara everything she wants. That's why I give her the car, the nose job, whatever she has asked for, I have found a way to give. I didn't think she needed a nose job by the way, but she wanted it, so I made it happen.

D: At the top of your list, Bradley, is self-esteem. How does Sara affect your self-esteem?

B: When she smiles, when she says thank you, when she holds me at night, when she cooks a nice meal, that feels good, that helps me feel special, that helps me feel I have value.

D: Sara, did you know that these acts helped Bradley feel these things that were so important?

S: (Smiles) No, actually I really didn't. I put romance high on my list. I was going to say the same thing about him. When he is kind to me, when he goes places with me, when he remembers our anniversary, or when he smiles at me first thing in the morning, those are the most romantic things in the world. Those things actually mean more to me than the gifts he gifts.

D: Bradley, did you know that?

B: No, I just assumed that the other gifts meant more. I didn't know that.

D: And for you, giving gifts was a way of being romantic and affectionate, correct?

B: Yes, that's what I thought a man should do.

S: I never asked you for that. Okay, I accepted the gifts. I enjoyed them. I won't deny that. But being with you, having you near me, having you go to my sister's wedding, means so much more.

D: Let's talk about that. I also notice that Sara ranked Family and Sociability fairly high on her list, while Bradley ranked Solitude and Quality Time high on his. I see some differences here.

S: I always thought it was weird he was such a loner.

B: I'm not a loner. I prefer smaller events or one-on-one time with someone instead of a huge party. I like having contact in a focused way. I've always been really uncomfortable at big parties and her family knows that.

D: I notice Self-Esteem is number one on your list, Bradley. Does Sara's family affect that for you?

B: Yes! That is another reason I don't want to go. Look, I'm sorry I can't deal with your toxic, messed up family. You can't even see how screwed up they are because you're so close to them. They really have some major problems. Plus, I only ever see each them at large family gatherings where I'm already nervous. Then they put me down.

S: They're not putting you down, they're making fun with you, not at you. It's their sense of humor. I know it's unusual but we all do it. By making fun they are including you, they're saying, "You're one of us."

B: Okay, fine, but I don't like it, I'm not comfortable with it. I don't feel like I'm one of them.

D: Sara, I notice you also listed Responsibility high on your list. So I'm going to ask you now truthfully, who is responsible for you having a good time at your sister's wedding?

S: I guess I am. I just know I would have a better time if he was by my side.

D: Maybe so. But does Responsibility mean you give Bradley or any one else one hundred percent of the power to determine how you feel?

S: No, if it did, that wouldn't be true responsibility.

D: Bradley, you claim that tolerance is high on your list, what does that mean to you?

B: Like it says on there, I respect the rights of people different from myself. I always vote for social change and equal rights.

D: Okay, but tolerance isn't only about political change. It is about how we live our personal lives as well. I have gotten the sense you have very little tolerance for Sara's family, their ways of communicating, their values that are different from yours, even their sense of humor. You claim that tolerance is important to you yet you condemn your in-laws for being different.

B: Okay, I get it, I don't like it, but I get it.

D: It seems that both of you at times have reacted to each other in ways that are outside of your stated integrity, and those actions have placed a profound amount of stress on the integrity pillar of your relationship. Consequently, you both came in here with both barrels loaded, shooting off verbal assaults and accusations at each other based on pent-up frustrations and resentments. In order to avoid further anger and attack, what can each of you do differently this week that would make your actions more consistent with your values?

As Sara and Bradley focus on strengthening their integrity pillar they will be able to rebuild their respect, appreciation and trust that was sorely missing in our first session.

Next they will able to focus on second pillar of rational relationship: Communication.

The Rational Relating Integrity Scale

Integrity is the consistency of one's actions in alignment with one's stated values or morals. When one or both partners say one thing and do another, this does significant damage to the relationship "pillar" and can lead to a collapse in the relationship. The scale below gives you an idea of how strong your integrity pillar is in your relationship today. Circle the number that corresponds best to your current situation.

1. There is a consistent pattern of lies, deceptions, and violations of agreements, allowing no ability to trust your partner. One or both partners frequently say one thing when they actually mean something different. There is very little pattern of stability and trust. Example: "I don't love you anymore, I want to break up," followed by "I do love you, I don't want to be without you."

2. There is an inconsistent follow-through with stated intentions, agreements and commitments, a general pattern of actions not matching stated values. At times one or both partners can stick to their words, and at other times they cannot. Example: Your partner has a pattern of both coming home on time, and not coming home on time, with very little predictability.

3. There is an overall consistency of actions matching stated values, with some exceptions. May include one or more significant violations of agreements in the past year. Examples: One person did something they agreed not to with another person outside of the relationship. Or both partners prioritize privacy but one snoops and reads the other's emails.

4. There is good consistency of actions matching stated values, with any violations minor and/or occasional. Example: Both members are trustworthy but occasionally one snaps at the other in a fit of anger. Both partners support each other but one misses an important event in the other's life.

5. A complete thread of consistency with actions that follow stated values, strong levels of trust between each partner. Exceptions to integrity are rare, and are easily forgiven. Example: Both partners follow through with verbal commitments, goals and agreements, though occasionally one may forget an anniversary, or accidentally disappoint the other.

CHAPTER FIVE

The Communication Pillar

D on and Kevin came to their evening appointment with noticeable tension between them. We had spent recent appointments exploring how each can improve his integrity, which included showing up on time for dates and meetings with one another. Consequently, they were both experiencing greater trust and appreciation in their three year relationship. But tonight something was definitely off.

"I'll start," Kevin said. "After everything we've talked about in here, after everything we have been through, you really let me down."

"I let *you* down?" Don shot back. "Are you kidding me? How can you sit there and pretend like everything is fine after what you did today?"

"Someone want to let me on this?" I asked.

Kevin responded, "I got a text from him this morning asking me if I wanted to do lunch today. It has been so long since we just slowed down and simply had lunch together so, of course, I said I would be there. He said to meet at our favorite place on 23rd street at 1st Ave so I rearranged my entire work schedule, showed up at noon, and what do you know, no Don. I waited and waited, no Don. I was hurt and angry."

Don looked puzzled. "I don't understand. That's not what I said at all." As both Don and Kevin quickly scrambled to look at their phones, they registered a look of concern, dread, and relief on both of their faces. "Now I get it," Don continued, "I texted you 'Let's meet at that place on 23rd at 1.' You thought I meant 1st avenue. I meant one o'clock in the afternoon."

★★★★★

The dearth of clear and effective communication is one of the greatest afflictions of our time. I can't tell you how many couples I have seen nearly breakup, divorce, and spend money on divorce lawyers, simply because of misunderstandings and incorrect assumptions. Professionally, I have seen jobs end, careers halt, and partnerships terminated, all because people simply did not effectively express themselves. There is no accounting for exactly how much time and energy is lost each year trying to rectify pain that stems from poor communication. But I can clearly pinpoint the difference it makes when two people begin to communicate rationally.

To make our Rational Communication pillar strong and long-lasting, we will need to learn and employ strategies and techniques that have been tested and proven. In this chapter, I will teach you the communication methods I have successfully used in hundreds of therapy sessions. They are all based in rational thinking, compassion for the other, and common sense. There is work involved—but the payoff is great, and can make a difference in *all* relationships in one's lifetime.

The alternative, poor or impaired communication, can be ruinous to relationships that might otherwise thrive. For example, Don and Kevin's misunderstanding above can be seen as an innocent error, but not unusual for couples who depend on texting for essential communications. As mentioned in Chapter One, technology enables us to have more contact than ever with our loved ones. Texting, chatting, tweeting, Skyping, and whatever comes next will allow people to share their every thought with others in seconds. Sadly, communication skills have not kept up with electronic opportunities, and relationships have paid the price.

There is no accounting for exactly how much time and energy is lost each year trying to rectify pain that stems from poor communication.

The word "communication" can have many different meanings and connotations. For the specific purpose of Rational Relating, "Communication" is defined by four components:

Clear Content—The skill of conveying one's inner thoughts and feelings in a manner that the intended recipient can understand. When you communicate you are trying to form and deepen a connection with another person by expressing an inner thought or feeling. That does little good if the person sitting across from you has no idea what are talking about. Learning how to give and receive information successfully so that your partner understands and receives your message is a challenge that even long term couples struggle with. But it can be done, and this chapter will offer specific tools and techniques for expressing your message clearly.

Consistent Expression—Just as the Integrity Pillar requires consistency in behavior based on personal values and beliefs, so does the Communication Pillar require the ability to express information, in tone as well as in word choice, consistent with your values. For instance, if you prioritize Compassion in your relationship, then you don't undermine it with words or tone by making disparaging or sarcastic remarks toward your partner or spouse. If you say you prioritize presence in your relationship, then you don't use your nonverbal communication—looking around, texting, appearing distracted—to convey that you'd rather be somewhere else.

Authentic Curiosity—Many partners in relationships want to be heard without making a mutual effort to reciprocate. Rational Communication is not only about expressing yourself effectively, it is about demonstrating an authentic and curious interest in what your partner is saying as well. Listening and hearing are distinctly different skills. Listening requires minimal involvement and engagement with your partner, and can easily be conveyed by parroting the other person's words back to them. Hearing, however, requires attention, presence, and empathy. Truly hearing what your partner is saying does not necessarily mean you agree, but it does mean that you strive to "get it" from their point of view, value their opinions, and communicate that understanding back to them.

Clarifying—It's always better to ask, even if the answer seems embarrassingly obvious. But even when you think you know the answer, as Kevin and Don demonstrated in their angry interaction above, you may not. Asking clarifying questions can enhance communication and express compassion for your partner. However, it also important that *how* you ask a question is consistent with your intention. "What do you think?" can be asked as a sarcastic dismissal or a gentle request, depending on the tone. When in doubt *ask* your partner how they heard your question, and *clarify* your intentions if your message is getting lost.

How Defense Will Damage

Questions that are intended to convey irritation or anger will most likely serve to break down connection and damage your Communication Pillar. These are examples of "defensive communications," i.e., words and expressions that result in your recipient feeling shamed, blamed, guilty, ridiculed, or defensive. Common examples of defensive questions are, "Why do you think that?" "You really want to know?" "See what you made me do?" "What is wrong with you?" and "Why are you so sensitive?"

This type of interaction has the cumulative effect of damaging pillars that are intended to support and maintain a satisfying relationship. After all, if your primary interactions with your partner results in one or both of you feeling sad, humiliated, or angry, why would you bother to communicate at all?

Some other common examples of defensive communication include:

- Use of sarcasm.
- Blaming the other person for how you feel.
- "You" statements, (i.e.—"You really blew it this time.")
- "Should" statements (i.e.—"You should clean up your mess.")

- "Why" questions (i.e.— "Why do you always do that?")
- Use of humor to convey aggression and anger.
- Use of tone of voice to convey a feeling different from the content of the words (i.e., "Aren't you the most thoughtful boyfriend ever," using a tone of voice that indicates you feel exactly the opposite)

Defensive communication makes up the majority of interactions in many relationships, and certainly accounts for about ninety percent of the exchanges between couples in my therapy office. This makes complete sense given that we live in a culture where people are not encouraged or rewarded for utilizing care and respect in their communication with others. Most of what people learn about communication involves the use of defensive communication strategies that give the illusion of power and control over others. But when it comes to intimate relationships, these techniques only serve to weaken the Communication Pillar, and do damage to the relationship structure.

When Humor Hurts

Have you ever had your feelings diminished by another person, only to be told, "It was just a joke, you shouldn't get so upset"? What happened? Did you suddenly feel a sense of levity and relief knowing that you had been harmed in the context of humor? Or did you feel like you had been reduced in a way that allowed the other person to play both sides, i.e., to mean it but not "really mean it"?

It is commonplace in our culture to use jokes as an "appropriate" way to mock groups of people based on religion, race, sexual orientation, and even gender. As laws discourage the use of hate speech, people often resort to "joking" to communicate a sense of distaste, disapproval, anger, and disgust. Sexual harassment, bullying, and even date rape often start out with aggressive language that is initially brushed off as "just a joke."

In relationships I have seen humor used to justify verbal cruelty and emotional abuse. When couples spend a considerable amount of time mocking each other's goals, dreams, appearance, families, or sexual patterns, it points to an unspoken level of aggression and poor communication skills.

Keep in mind, there can be plenty of laughter, fun, joking, and playful banter in relationships. The key element is *consent*. Just like any physical act, without tacit consent and agreement, the "joking" is aggression. Couples in Rational Relationships are encouraged to discuss what is acceptable to joke about, and what is not. One person's crazy aunt might be completely fair game for making fun, while another person's mentally disturbed brother may not.

Either way, it is every couple's responsibility to determine what is and what isn't appropriate for humorous fodder. When there is misunderstanding in this area, it leads to hurtful feelings, angry reactions, and significant damage to the relationship pillars. Here are some tips for using humor to increase connection instead of separation:

- When in doubt, ask your partner if laughing about something would be funny or hurtful.
- If the humor relates to a current event (an illness, a pregnancy, a life change) then check in with your partner consistently to make sure it is still okay to joke about it.
- Asking for permission doesn't diminish the joke. If you are truly funny, you will find a way to find humor within the consented agreements and boundaries.
- If you do end up getting hurt by your partner's banter, use the Effective Communication tools in this chapter to tell them.
- Respect the fact that your partner's friends and family may have different boundaries and guidelines around your humor, and a different context for knowing you. When in doubt, withhold the joke.

Rational Communication Strategies

Communication in Rational Relating is carried out with the intention of expressing thoughts, feelings, and information to another person in a manner that conveys respect, compassion, and appreciation for the other. Although you have no control over how someone receives your message, you do get a say in your intention. Here are some tools and ideas for effectively communicating in a relationship:

Use "I" Statements: When stating an opinion, a preference, or even a rational criticism/concern, it behooves the relationship to begin your comment with an "I" statement. Use of the word "I" puts in context your perspective as a speaker, as opposed to expressing an ominous worldwide truth. For instance, there is a difference between saying, "You made a mess," versus, "I would like you to clean up the mess you made." By using "I" you are assuming ownership and responsibility for your point of view, which also reinforces the Responsibility Pillar (coming in Chapter Seven).

Replace the "Should": As mentioned earlier, the word "should" functions primarily to induce a sense of shame in one's partner and establish yourself as a superior authority. For example, when Sara said to Bradley, "A husband should go to a family wedding with his wife," what was Bradley's response? Did he relax and say, "Oh, you have a point"? No, like most people Bradley met the "should" with defense, anger, and a deepened resignation to do the exact opposite of what he was being told he should do by his wife.

An example of Rational Communication would have been for Sara to say, "It would mean a lot to me if you went. It would be wonderful to have you by my side on this special day. I enjoy spending time with you. You make these events that much better." See a difference? In the latter example, Sara would be taking full responsibility for her feelings and presenting her preferences in a way that could very well open Bradley's mind and heart. She is not passing judgment about what a husband "should" do, she is sincerely sharing her personal experience. This level of rational communication does wonders for compromise as well.

Apply The Agreement Technique: You find something, anything, to agree with in the content the other person is saying. For instance, if a client tells me I'm the Worst Therapist Ever, I have two choices. Using defense communication I could defend myself as a professional, use hundreds of clients as examples of how great I am, use my books to prove that I'm credible, and then place the problem one hundred percent on the client for not appreciating my infallible talents.

Or, I could simply say, "Yeah, sometimes I suck."

The latter response serves several purposes. First, it gets the client and myself out of the irrational "all or nothing" cycle that fuels extreme statements like, "You're the worst (anything)." I may be off sometimes but the worst, probably not. Nevertheless, I'm sure I fall somewhere in the continuum of great and sucky and have no problem admitting that I've had my moments of both. By demonstrating the flexibility of thinking in shades of gray, instead of black/white, I am actually disproving the client's argument on the spot.

That response also serves to end the adrenaline-filled fight in the client's head. When someone in a personal or professional context comes at you in an irrational way, you certainly have the right to defend yourself by opposing them. But doing so usually increases their resistance to you, and strengthens their convictions against you. This point cannot be emphasized enough when it comes to Rational Communication. Whenever you defend against something you easily create more of the very thing you are defending against.

Have you ever watched two people arm wrestle? What happens? They start evenly and then they push against each other. What happens to all the muscles in their arms as they struggle? As they resist the pressure of the other those muscles get stronger and bigger. The same thing happens when you and another person get into an arguing match. Every time you argue defensively, you strengthen the other person's resistance and you force them to become more solid in their beliefs and feelings against you.

Ask Clarifying Questions: Once again, you can often improve communication and deepen your connections with others by asking authentic questions that are relevant to what the other person is saying. For instance, Doreen would come home from work frustrated, stressed, and upset by problems at work. Her husband Jim loved her tremendously, couldn't stand to see her upset, and responded to her complaints by going into "fix-it" mode, trying to convey his love and concern by problem solving.

Doreen, on the other hand, did not need or want a fix or a solution, she just wished to share her struggles with the man she loved the most. At times, she experienced Jim's problem solving as invasive and insensitive. "Sometimes he has some really valid points. There are times I want him to shut up and not say anything. But then he does say something and more often than not what he says actually does help with the problem."

"Now I'm really confused," Jim replied. "I don't know what you want. A warm shoulder to cry on, or practical advice?"

"Well, if you're not sure, you could ask me," Doreen said.

Like a light bulb, Jim's confusion was cleared up. He later expressed "relief" at no longer having to decipher the intricacies of Doreen's mood, her complaints, her tone of voice, and her body language to know what she needed. He could simply ask her, "What do you prefer from me right now? Just to listen, or to offer some ideas?"

So often people will struggle to speculate, analyze, and evaluate what a partner or spouse wants. They'll do everything except just ask the person what they want. I have heard many say, "I've been with her for so long, I should just know by now without asking." The problem is, people's needs change all the time. By asking honest and authentic questions you increase your sensitivity, demonstrate interest, and increase bonds with the person you are asking.

Express "Thank You" Statements: One of the most universal aspects of relationships is the desire and need to be appreciated. No matter how new or old the union, in what culture or part of the world, there is a basic human drive to experience gratitude and acknowledgment from a partner.

The use of "thank yous" in daily life cannot be overestimated in Rational Communication. "Thank you" is basically saying, "I see you, I notice you, I appreciate you, I'm grateful to you." If couples used this technique consistently, I am convinced there would be much less need for therapists and divorce lawyers. The act of saying "thank you" is so minimal, while the impact is phenomenal. Regular use of "thank yous" have been known to increase intimacy, diminish arguing, and repair long-standing damage done to pillars over time.

Unfortunately, most people are conditioned to express grievances over gratitude. Most have been taught that it is more effective to complain about a partner than appreciate them. They have the idea that they are more likely to get what they want when they judge a loved one instead of value them.

This conditioning has been detrimental to relationships in all times. Long-term Rational Relationships that promote growth, joy, and serenity are steadily rooted in unabashed gratitude. This does not mean you love and agree with everything your partner says and does. You do not become a "doormat" when you say "thank you." You simply maintain a position of humble appreciation that this person is alive and he is spending time with you. In my experience, couples that can maintain this stance spend less time arguing and more time resolving differences in creative rational ways.

Display Consistent Tone of Voice and Gestures with Words: It is one thing to speak words, it is quite another to mean them. The use of sarcasm and irony—that is the deliberate use of a tone of voice that juxtaposes the content of words—does little to promote trust, consistency, and growth in a relationship. For example, if one partner says, "I'm sorry you feel that way" to the other in a sincere manner, this will result in the other partner feeling recognized, appreciated, cherished, and more likely to forgive. If a partner says the same phrase with his tone of voice undermining the sincerity of the words, then this will most likely result in the partner feeling shamed, embarrassed, judged, and less inclined to want to communicate in the future.

Why do people say one thing when they mean another? Typically this tool is employed when one feels powerless. Adolescents often become experts in the use of sarcasm and irony when they are in a situation where there is a power imbalance. Whether it's a teacher, parent, or some authority figure, teenagers will often betray the content of their words with their tone of voice in order to resist feeling oppressed. It is a resilient, albeit ineffective, way to equalize the playing field, and experience brief moments of empowerment.

Adults frequently employ the same technique in similar situations. When someone feels underappreciated or exploited by a person in a position of power, she will often use sarcasm to "turn the tables" in order to maintain a sense of dignity. As a former waiter, I can't count the number of times I said, "It's been a pleasure to serve you," when my tone conveyed it was anything but. When one is feeling dehumanized, with no recourse or outlet to communicate their feelings, then this type of communication will instinctively seep through.

Similarly, many use non-verbal gestures to convey that they do not mean what they are saying. Eye rolling, insincere smiles, a raise of the eyebrow—all are unspoken expressions which communicate, "I didn't mean what I just said to you." An abundance of these physicalities, along with tone of voice, can be detrimental to Rational Communication.

Again, we do not live in a society where effective, respectful, and honorable communication is the norm. Respect, compassion, and appreciation are not abundant gifts in this world, and our typical communication patterns are reflective of this deficit. And then we wonder why half of all marriages end in divorce. Without a strong Communication Pillar, the structure of the relationship can be quite strained. If your verbal messages are confusing, contradictory and heard as punishing, then you may inadvertently be shaming or hurting the one you love, and breaking down the possibility of future communication.

Know Your "Audience": With all that having been said, I fully acknowledge that there can be a time and place for anything. There may in fact be times when sarcasm or irony can be used for bonding and connecting. The trick is having the context set up with someone you already know.

When I am preparing for a speaking engagement or lecture, I do my absolute best to make sure I know who my audience is. Although my message is the same wherever I go, my method does vary. My attitude and tone will tend to be more relaxed if I am talking to a group of stressed-out case managers in a non-profit service organization than if I'm talking to a group of CPAs in a corporate accounting firm. I may use selective curse words and explicit humor if I'm speaking at a social event for polyamorous couples, but not in a Sunday morning talk at a local spiritual organization. In any example, I know my audience and tailor my communication accordingly.

In Rational Relationships, the same sensible judgment applies. There may be times when you and your partner communicate in a way that it is light-hearted, humorous, sarcastic, and silly. Remember, Rational Relationships are about creating, not conforming, which means each and every couple may have their own set of nuances, inside jokes, and/or physical gestures, that may in context serve to promote love, respect, and appreciation. Prior communication and understanding are the keys. Without them, the potential for damaging misunderstandings is greatly increased.

So how do you know? Once again, ask. For example, if your partner is an actress, and you make a comment about actresses not knowing the difference between life on and off camera, then it is in service of your Communication Pillar that you ask your partner how she feels about such a statement. She may be one hundred percent in agreement and think that is an insightful and brilliant observation. Or she may take offense, get defensive, and withdraw from communicating with you, or employ the use of sarcasm to "balance out" the power. Either way, you don't know unless you ask.

I would go so far as to recommend asking even when you think you know. In the previous example, even if she nods and registers an "oh you are so right" expression on her face, she still may be thinking, "What an ass, why would he say that?" Words and judgments can still be received criticisms and condemnations unless you know your "audience" through asking questions.

The Five Prior Agreements of Rational Communication

All the aforementioned tools can be sabotaged if certain guidelines are not followed. I strongly encourage couples to look over these ideas, and if they make sense, make a serious agreement to follow them.

1. **No serious discussions under the influence of drugs or alcohol.** Remember, the foundation of Rational Relating is rationality. If a substance affects your brain, then your ability to think and speak rationally is affected as well. I cannot tell you how many couples' relationship pillars have been devastated when trying to have a serious discussion while drunk or high. An easier and more respectful way is for both to agree: If we are altering our mood with a substance, we do not discuss "third rail" issues. If something really important comes up at these times, then write it down and bring it up when sober and rational.

2. **No serious issues discussed through texts, e-chats, e-mails.** Technology presents us with wonderful opportunities to connect. But it does not offer us wonderful opportunities to communicate. "Can you pick up some milk for me if you're going by the store?" is a perfectly appropriate

text. "I love you and am thinking about you" is a wonderful sentiment for an email. "I am so grateful for you in my life" is a beautiful statement for an e-chat. But, "I've been thinking about our relationship and there are things we need to talk about" is not. This use of technology only leads to stress, confusion, anger, and anxiety.

3. **Employ the use of time-outs.** Young children in play yards are well familiar with the effective use of time-outs. They essentially communicate, "You are not yourself right now. Take a breather and come back when you can play nice." This guideline would be wisely followed by adults when emotional adrenaline appears to be overwhelming, and words are being used that are not truly meant. A structured "time-out" period can save "time in" the therapy office.

4. **Don't assume.** This has been touched upon many times in this book, and will be mentioned again. The reason it is repeated so many times is because it is so darn easy for us to forget. It is our nature to make sense of things in our mind so we don't have to think hard. In mathematics, we are relieved that 2+2= 4. Every time. But in Rational Relationships we consistently ask questions and check with the other person to make sure that what was true last month is still true now (i.e., we're getting married + she's not working = she's happy). Check consistently, ask frequently!

5. **No "Drop and Runs."** It is unacceptable in a Rational Relationship to declare, "I have to talk to you about something important" and then run off, hang up the phone, sign off from Facebook, or somehow cut off communication. It is a passive aggressive maneuver that leaves the other person emotionally hanging for hours or days at a time, usually leading to anxiety, stress, and resentment. The other person then has to spend

the interval of time playing a guessing game of what that Big Thing is you want to discuss.

In therapy we call this the "Drop and Run," because you are dropping a bomb of sorts, and leaving the other person holding all the confusion and uncertainty. In a Rational Relationship it is much more humane to wait until an undistracted and unrushed time to bring up important matters. Or, if circumstances make this impossible, you can preface it with, "Everything is fine, but I just need some time with you." You are then communicating in a way that serves to protect the integrity of your relationship, and not cause your partner unnecessary worry.

The Apology Controversy

The value of an apology comes up frequently in couples therapy. On one hand, a sincere apology can be an indelible part of repairing damage to a relationship's structure. But when it is not expressed authentically, it can betray a sense of resentment, entitlement, and condescension. How do you know when an apology will help or hinder? It depends on whether it is sincere or insincere, and whether or not the apologizer actually acted outside of their integrity or not (as described in Chapter Four).

When someone says or does something outside their stated values they are operating outside of their integrity. The physical and emotional consequences of behaving outside of integrity often have devastating consequences for one's partner. The diagram below outlines the four different apologies that can occur when this happens:

	Sincere	Insincere
Person acted outside of integrity	"I am so sorry about what I did and how it hurt you. If I could take it back I would. Help me understand how to make it better."	"I made a mistake. I'm sorry you are making such a big deal about it"
Person acted inside of integrity	"I'm not sorry about what I did, but I am truly sorry that my actions resulted in hurting you. Help me understand how to make it better."	"This is your problem. I'm sorry you are struggling with it."

Randy and Lynn's conflict will illustrate these scenarios. Randy is a hardworking lawyer in a corporate firm, trying to move his way up and demonstrate he is partner material. Lynn works as a teacher, and has been looking forward to celebrating their one year wedding anniversary. She plans a romantic dinner at home, with Randy's favorite foods and decorations, and looks forward to sharing a special night with her husband. Randy, meanwhile, gets ordered to stay late to work on a major case. He tells Lynn earlier in the day he will be delayed, only to realize by 5pm that he won't be home for several hours, thereby missing their anniversary dinner. Lynn is devastated.

There are four different ways an apology can be expressed:

Randy acted outside his integrity / sincere apology: "I am so profoundly sorry for what I did. It was wrong, it was hurtful, I don't feel good about it, and I'm devastated how much I've hurt you. I want to make this right with you, and hope we can talk about how to repair this going forward."

Randy acted inside his integrity / sincere apology: "I am so sorry my decision hurt you, it hurt me too. I did what I honestly believed I had to do. But it devastates me that my actions affected you so badly. I want to make this right with you, and hope we can talk about how to repair this going forward."

Randy acted outside his integrity / insincere apology: "Okay, I messed up, but you are making way too big a deal about this. I know it was wrong to stay so late at work, but you should know that's part of my job and how I keep money coming in. I'm sorry that upsets you so much."

Randy acted inside his integrity / insincere apology: "I have done nothing wrong. This is my job. I don't see why you're making such a big deal about it. I'm sorry you're having such a hard time with this."

As you can see, some apologies are going to be more effective in repairing damage to a relationship's structure than others. Of course the impact of the apology will also be affected by Randy's nonverbal communication, tone of voice, history of having done similar things in the past, and Lynn's willingness to forgive.

This is not to say that a sincere apology solves the problem and erases hurt feelings. It may introduce new questions about differences in integrity and values. Lynn may come away from this aware that Randy's work comes first and he does have integrity (consistency) around that. She can then use the tools in this book to communicate effectively about her feelings utilizing the skills of compassion, responsibility, and compromise that are outlined in future chapters.

It is clear that the sincere apologies (as in the examples above) are more likely to be reparative to a structure than insincere apologies. Sincere apologies integrate compassion and collaboration, even if the person does not see themselves as having done something "wrong." Insincere apologies create a dynamic of dismissal and disregard, and do considerable damage to the relationship structure.

Rational Communication Exercises

There can be several ways to practice these ideas with your partner that promote intimacy, connection, and growth. Below are some tools I have used successfully in my practice.

"Thank You" Exercise: Before you go to sleep, you each thank the other for five things. They can be for smaller things like, "Thank you for taking out the trash." Bigger things like, "Thank you for taking me out to my favorite meal." Or large things like,

"Thank you for being my best friend." You can mix them all together if preferred.

"I Love You" Exercise: Similar to the "Thank you" exercise, except this time you complete the sentence, "I love you because _____."

"How Are You Feeling?" Exercise: This is especially effective when couples are in the habit of assuming they know what the other person is thinking and feeling. They often forget to ask each other how the other is doing. I ask couples to do this exercise at least once a day, more than that if they are spending time together on a weekend or vacation. At various intervals you turn to your partner, and simply ask, "How are you feeling right now?" Even if you think you know the answer. If your partner has a response you are not expecting, refrain from condemning or judging. Instead, try asking more explorative questions:

"Do you know why you are feeling that way?"

"Would you like to tell me more?"

"What can I do to help?"

"Shoulds for Dollars" Exercise: Both members agree on a moratorium of "shoulds" for a stated period of time. It could be a day, a week, a year, a lifetime, whatever you and your partner agree upon. During this period of time, the use of "shoulds" against the other is banned. If one partner uses "should" they have to give the other a dollar. If you want to raise the stakes, you can increase it to five dollars or even twenty. The purpose of this is to realize that "shoulds" do much damage to relationship pillars, often in ways that are not immediately noticeable. When you have to pay cash for "shoulds" you are instantly reminded that "shoulds" have consequences for yourself and the relationship you want to preserve.

These exercises worked wonders for Glenn and Maria, a young couple considering marriage, who came in to see me because of "tension" in their relationship. It was soon revealed in our first session that Maria was three months pregnant with Glenn's child and experiencing much confusion about the direction of their relationship. She could acknowledge she loved Glenn and believed he would make a great father. But the fact that he was frequently jobless, lacked career direction, and failed to fulfill basic commitments around the house concerned her. Furthermore, her own mood swings and "rage fits" were increasing, and she did not wish to subject Glenn to abuse or emotional violence.

On Glenn's end, he expressed feeling "thrilled" with being a father, and wanting very much to get married and spend his life with Maria. But her "Latina temper" combined with "crazy hormones" concerned him, as well as his own financial situation. He had obtained a Master of Fine Arts in Design but had no idea what he wanted to do with it.

Over our first few sessions I gave Glenn and Maria all of the above exercises as homework assignments (as well as the Rational Inventory of Values list from Chapter Four). They were told one week that they had to list five things they loved about the other before they went to sleep at night. Then they had to say "I love you because _____" several times during the day.

The next week they agreed to ask more questions about how the other is thinking and feeling. It was revealed during this time that Maria did not appreciate the stereotype of having a "Latina temper," as she felt it was not only racially offensive, but diminished the validity of her emotions. She rationally conveyed this to Glenn by stating: "I don't feel good when you put me into a category like that. It is offensive, dehumanizing, and only results in me getting angrier. My anger is confusing, but it is real, and it is personally my own." Glenn took full responsibility for his words, and agreed not to knowingly use pejorative language again. He added, "I don't always know how my words impact you unless you tell me. Will you agree to let me know if I accidentally say something offensive again?" Maria indicated she would.

"One more question," Glenn replied. "Are you offended or hurt when I use the term 'crazy hormones'?"

"No," Maria laughed, "That's okay, they really are crazy right now."

By doing these exercises, Glenn and Maria were able to change a pattern of complaints and fault seeking into a pattern of gratitude and appreciation. With that in mind they could go forward with asking each other questions and having conversations that promoted clarity and the sense that they are on the same "team."

Next I gave them the "Shoulds for Dollars" exercise. They agreed to follow that, and came back the next week holding hands and touching legs during session. "The entire week I felt accepted by him," Maria said. "Whether I was laughing, crying, or both at the same time, I felt there were no 'shoulds' about how I was feeling or what I was doing, and that Glenn was going to be my friend no matter what. Plus I made ten bucks!"

Soon after, Glenn got a job with a website that would allow him to do some design, and also work at home a great amount of time. "It's not my dream job," he said, "but it works for now." The improved communication, clarity, and focus on gratitude, enabled Glenn and Maria to deepen intimacy, appreciation, and express the love for each other and their child that was consistent with their integrity.

The Biggest Obstacle to Communication: "I Shouldn't Have To" (aka "I SH-T")

If you are like most, the emphasis on asking questions, expressing gratitude, and rationally communicating may seem excessive. There may have been times during this chapter that you've thought, "I shouldn't have to do this with someone I love," or "I shouldn't have to do this after being married for so many years," or "I shouldn't have to say 'thank you'," or "I shouldn't have to ask for what I want. If they love me they'll just know."

There is a good reason why the acronym for "I shouldn't have to" is "I SH-T." Declaring that you or your partner shouldn't have to say or do something is metaphorically soiling your relationship pillars. It is saying your relationship doesn't matter very much, that it is not worthy of attention, focus, and time intensive work.

Anyone who has ever gone to the gym consistently and gotten into shape knows that physical fitness is a lifelong process. You don't just work out for six months consistently and say, "I'm good now, no more of that for me." Similarly, anyone who has ever kept up a garden is well aware of the time, focus, and energy demanded of plants, trees, and flowers. Maybe you "should not have to" invest so much effort in having a toned body or beautiful flowers and plants, but many do it anyway because they know they will not see their desired results if they don't.

Relationships work exactly the same way. They are a constant ever-changing dynamic that consistently demand attention, nurturing, strengthening, and reinforcing. It doesn't work to say, "I gave my girlfriend lots of attention and praise that first year so she shouldn't still need it to know how much I love her now." Rational Relating is based on the premise that even the strongest of pillars need reinforcement now and then. "I shouldn't have to" consistently wears down pillars over time.

It doesn't work to say, "I gave my girlfriend lots of attention and praise that first year so she shouldn't still need it to know how much I love her now."

If you want your relationship to last, you will consider eliminating "I shouldn't have to," and replace it with "I'm going to." Instead of saying, "I shouldn't have to tell him how much I appreciate him," you replace it with, "I'm going to tell him how much I appreciate him." Instead of saying, "I shouldn't have to reassure her that I'm thinking about her while I'm visiting my mother," you say, "I'm going to reassure her that I'm thinking about her while I'm visiting my mother." These small yet vital gestures do immeasurable reparation to relationship pillars that have been worn down over time.

Sara and Bradley on Communication

SARA (S): I don't see how this therapy is helping. He's still not going to my sister's wedding. He's still chatting with Melissa online. He's still doesn't do the things a husband should.

BRADLEY (B): And she still expects that I'm going to work day and night to give her some quality of life that she doesn't even want? That's crazy. (To Sara) Look, you are so selfish, so ungrateful, so miserable all the time, that I can't imagine any man putting up with you more than I have. And as long as your family is involved I can guarantee you that no real man will get near you.

S: Good, because if you're a "real man" then I'm Mother Teresa.

DAMON (D): So time-out for a moment. Sara, how do you feel right now?

S: Angry, upset, discouraged.

D: On a scale of 1-10, with 10 being the most, how much do you believe this marriage can be saved?

S: At this moment, about a "3."

D: Bradley what are you feeling right now?

B: That I want to get the hell away from her.

D: Actually "I want to get the hell away from her" is a thought. Can you name a feeling behind the thought?

B: I'm pissed, I'm frustrated, I'm angry.

D: And on a scale of 1-10, how much do you believe this marriage can be saved?

B: "2."

D: Okay, next I want to try something that is going to seem weird but go with me here. I want you both to sit up straight, with both feet on the floor, take a deep breath, and as you breathe I want you to remember something you love about the other. It can be based on a memory from the past, something about their looks, anything you can recall right now that is loving about the other. Sara, I want you to face Bradley and tell him three things you love about him right now.

S: Three things? Okay. Bradley, I love your glasses. I have always thought your glasses were so cute. I love the way you dance around to your old Nirvana CDs. And I love that you want to give me everything you think I want. That is very kind.

D: Okay, Bradley, your turn, to Sara.

B: Sara, I love that you don't take crap from anyone in your life. I wish I could be more like that sometimes. I love when you make chicken parm with the perfect amount of cheese on top. You never skimp on the cheese. And I love that your smile is the first thing I see when I put my cute glasses on in the morning. (They both laugh).

D: And how does that feel?

B: I feel good right now.

S: Yeah, so do I.

D: And what just changed?

B: Remembering the reasons we got together in the first place. Remembering the little things that are still really good.

S: Yeah, it's like I feel better about him when I appreciate these things. It's easy to forget about them.

D: Sara, at this exact moment on a scale of 1-10, how much to you believe this marriage can be saved?

S: At this moment it's more of a "7."

B: Me too.

D: So you both just demonstrated the ability to change your mood at any time simply by communicating. This is a rational tool I use because it's an immediate reminder that there is more to your spouse than just problems. The problems you two are experiencing are only one part of an intricate system of joy, pleasure, happiness, and yes, at times disappointment and frustration. But it is never all one-or-the-other. Does that make sense?

This session would then be followed up with homework assignments that would increase and improve Rational Communication at home as well. By practicing these exercises Sara and Bradley are both able to experience an increase in appreciation, gratitude, and faith that the marriage pillars will hold up.

The Rational Relating Communication Scale

Communication in a Rational Relationship is carried out with the intention of conveying thoughts, feelings, and information to another person in a manner that conveys respect, compassion, and appreciation for the other's humanity. This scale below give you an idea of how strong your relationship's communication pillar is today. Circle the number that corresponds best to your current situation:

1. One or both members use defensive / hostile communication styles to convey feelings, thoughts, and beliefs. This can include name-calling, blame, violent language, hate speech, "you" statements, sarcasm, and questions for the sake of making a point (instead of curiously seeking knowledge).

2. Most words and interactions are accusatory, with some means of Rational Communication at times. Hostile defensive epithets may be interspersed with sincere "I love yous."

3. Some use of rational communication, while words may not match up with tone or attitude, (i.e., saying "You're so thoughtful" while sounding annoyed and irritated). Use of defensive styles still present. There is a consistent mix of both defensive examples and rational examples.

4. Overall good use of rational communication styles, with some occasional defensive patterns, and/or attack speech. For example, one may practice "I" statements and ask genuine questions, but at times use "shoulds" and "you" statements when provoked.

5. Consistent use of effective verbal communication patterns that convey respect, gratitude, appreciation, and love for the other partner. Tone and and attitude match with words. Use of defensive styles, if present, is scarce and minor.

CHAPTER SIX

The Compassion Pillar

Compassion can best be described as a way of acknowledging and recognizing the humanity in others, and then making your best effort not to inflict misery or suffering on those others. It can be an action, an intention, and a general willingness "to do no intended harm." Compassion demonstrates a basic and fundamental respect for the value of human lives, and guides you as to how to react or not react in interactions with loved ones.

In Rational Relating terms, compassion is used when you question the distorted thought patterns described in Chapter Three and change those beliefs that lead to your own unhappiness. After all, a compassionate person does not promote suffering in others, beginning with him or herself. It is not compassionate and therefore cruel to inflict harmful ideas against oneself such as, "I'm no good," "I'm too old," "I'm completely unlovable," "I'm a complete failure," "Nothing ever works out for me," or, "Everything is always going to go horribly wrong for the rest of my life." These and other such irrational thoughts can lead to prolonged depression, guilt, anger, anxiety, and a host of other feelings that exacerbate suffering.

To be clear, there is a difference between "pain" and "suffering." Pain is the unavoidable feeling that you inevitably experience from time to time if you are truly living and loving in this world. If you love someone who dies, you will emotionally feel pain. If someone comes over and hits you, then you will physically feel pain. The "suffering," however, is completely optional.

Suffering is the avoidable experience that results from what you tell yourself about the pain. After a death, if you say to yourself, "That shouldn't have happened," "That was a terrible thing," "That was unfair," or "What's the point in loving others, they're all going to leave me anyway," then you will suffer. If someone hits you and you tell yourself, "I should have prevented that," "I'm such an idiot for allowing that to happen," "Why wouldn't someone hit a loser like me," then you will suffer.

Compassion can be an action, an intention, and a general willingness "to do no intended harm to others."

It is impossible to live in this world without occasionally causing pain to others. You may not be romantically interested in someone who has feelings for you. You may move away from a tight family or community who miss you every day. You may leave a job where you have customers and clients who have become attached to you.

But compassion means you do not *intentionally* seek to cause suffering to others. You don't use words that would knowingly harm another person. You don't turn down someone's romantic advances by saying, "Not in a million years, loser!" You don't leave your caring community and family by saying, "I can't wait to get away from you people." You don't leave a job where you will be missed by saying, "I'll forget you by next week."

Similarly, being in relationships with others means you will inevitably cause pain to the other person at times. Misunderstandings happen, feelings get hurt. Sometimes people have two very different ambitions and goals. It's not a question of "if" this will happen, it is a matter of "when" and how a couple chooses to manage it. When there are already strong pillars of integrity and communication, then violations of compassion can be more easily navigated. But there are techniques and tools to enhance and reinforce the Compassion Pillar as well.

Sharing The P.I.P.E. of Rational Compassion

How, then, does one build and maintain the Compassion Pillar in a Rational Relationship? It involves sharing the "P.I.P.E." of Rational Compassion—Presence, Impermanence, Patience, and Empathy.

Presence: I love to watch people in public places, especially in restaurants. It has now become so commonplace to see couples sit down a table, have a sip of water, and then immediately take out their phones and type away. I'm always tempted to ask, "Are either one of you *here* right now?"

Of course I have no way of knowing if their distraction translates into other contexts. And for all I know, they could be sitting there texting or IM-ing each other. But what is clear in the 21st Century is that the interest and skill to engage in a face-to-face conversation without a mechanical object buzzing, humming, ringing, or singing is fading.

As I mentioned in Chapter Two, I often wonder if part of the consistent allure of therapy is that people get what they can't get anywhere else: Presence. Presence is the state of being one hundred percent focused on the other person with your mind, body, heart, and spirit. It is prioritizing the other person sitting in front of you in order to convey that they are important, valuable, relevant, vital, and essential. It is a way of listening that allows you to absorb the other person's words, thoughts, and emotions without focusing on the past or the future. It is a way of being available for someone in the *now*.

I have found it has become increasingly rare to find and maintain presence in a world that normalizes and validates distraction. It once was considered rude to take a call in the middle of a meal with another person. It once was considered insensitive to carry on a conversation with one or more people online while you are sitting face-to-face with a loved one.

As presence becomes more of a scarcity in society, it is even more cherished in primary relationships. By giving your partner undivided time and clear focus, you are giving him or her a gift unlike any other. Remaining present in your relationship increases intimacy, understanding, connection, and goes a long way to strengthen the compassion pillar.

Impermanence: There is no such thing as a permanent relationship. None. Everything, at some point, will end. It may be a year, a decade, or fifty years from now, but every relationship has a finite date.

The 14th Dalai Lama, Tenzin Gyatso, has spoken openly and frequently about the impermanence of relationships. They will all end because no life form lasts forever. The one thing that all humans have in common is the fact that at some point we are going to die. Facing that fact is simply rational, or as The Dalai Lama says, "realistic."

This perspective, however, does not have to be a downer. In fact, facing the reality of impermanence can fuel a sense of meaning in every given moment you spend with your partner. It can also remind you how fragile and finite life can be. Time is not to be wasted on petty disputes and shallow grievances. Every minute of every day counts; it's up to you to decide how you want to invest your precious time.

This is especially relevant for couples who are getting married, or have recently gotten married. The institution of marriage suggests that a relationship is somehow "permanent," and that the two people involved have infinite years ahead of them. Anyone who has ever gone through a breakup, a divorce, or death of a loved one knows that there are never any guarantees.

Time is not to be wasted on petty disputes and shallow grievances.

What if you knew for certain that you only had a week left with the person you love the most? What, if anything, would you do differently? Would you use kinder words when addressing him? Would you be more thoughtful and attentive to her needs? Would you savor every moment that you two spend together? You don't have to wait to make this happen, you can practice Rational

Compassion by accepting impermanence and incorporating appreciation for the scarcity of time now.

Patience: As a young child I have clear memories of going to the bank with my mother and having to wait in a long line. This was before there were any ATMs or electronic means to get cash. You had to go to a location, park a car, walk inside, wait in line, talk to a bank teller, wait for them to look up your account, and then give you money. This could take anywhere from 10 to 30 minutes, depending on how many other people were waiting to do the same thing. During that time, my mother and I would talk, play games, occasionally laugh with other people. I learned from her that waiting time can be quality time. Can you imagine waiting that long to get money today? I, for one, get in a huff if I have to wait two minutes to use an ATM. What happened to patience?

From fast food to rapid communication to instant entertainment, we want, and expect, everything to happen quickly without a wait. When something you use gets old and outdated you can easily replace it with a newer model. The computer I am using to write this book is now four years old and already its features and original software are completely outdated. That, in and of itself, is not necessarily a "bad" thing. It is when we translate a feeling of entitlement to new and immediate gratification into our relationships that we can do damage.

Despite advances in technology, humans are still slow animals when it comes to truly getting to know a significant other. Understanding their mood swings, their sleeping patterns, their habits, their voice patterns, their speech rhythms, their reactions to stress and frustrations, their managing of disappointments, their ability to hold friendships and relationships with others, their health, their beliefs, their abilities to manage money, their abilities to hold a job, their fluctuating sex drives, all come with time. There is no downloadable app to make this happen.

All too often, I see people approaching relationships the same way they approach technology. They meet someone, get swept up in the "new relationship energy," think they've met the "right one," and declare undying love. A few months later, the relationship isn't so new and shiny, they refer to the other person as "boring," they report feeling disappointed, and move on to the next toy. There is no patience in this scenario, no pacing, no time allowed to cultivate and nurture a real connection that may outlast the "next model."

Despite advances in technology, humans are still slow animals when it comes to truly getting to know a significant other.

Or, even in longer term couples, I have seen people wanting to run at the first sign of strife. When a partner goes through a mental or physical illness, gains weight, or goes through a financial downfall, the other person wants to jump ship and state, "I just can't deal with this." This knee-jerk reaction to ending a relationship lacks patience, compassion, and is often outside of one's integrity.

With patience, people are able to wait longer and make decisions that are more deliberate, conscientious, and clear. It doesn't mean that every couple decides to stay together, but with patience each person does get the opportunity to gain understanding, experience closure, and enter into the next part of their life with less "baggage."

Empathy: Some have asked me why empathy is not a pillar unto itself. For me, empathy simply means you have the ability to see things from another person's point of view. There is nothing inherently compassionate about that. As a matter of fact, empathy can be used for just the opposite in interpersonal relationships. When you can see things from another person's perspective, you have the ability to know exactly how to push their buttons and hurt them where they are most vulnerable.

However, the empathy that I hope to illustrate here is the kind that is used to reinforce compassion, not enable manipulation. Empathy allows you to see the world through another's eyes, heart, and values. When you have been intimate with someone who really "gets you," it not only enables you to experience a profound connection with another person, but it also alleviates fears of being alone in a confusing world.

Like patience and presence, empathy is becoming more and more scarce on a cultural level. Politically, we are seeing more extreme groups gain momentum, on both the right and the left, whose ideologies appear to eclipse any sense of empathy or understanding for people who don't completely agree with their values. Medically we are seeing efforts that would help all Americans have access to decent health care continuously face obstacles. Financially, a long term recession had led to a scarcity of economic resources which has led many to focus narrowly on "me" instead of "we." True empathy is getting harder and harder to come by, and at the same time, is becoming increasingly treasured in interpersonal relationships.

To give and receive the gift of loving empathy is a blessing. It is an essential and fundamental part of the compassion pillar which helps to keep a relationship strong and unshakable even under the stress of problems and emotional "disasters."

The Scoop on Snoop

It would be easier if I could write "Just don't snoop" and have that be enough. Snooping only leads to pain, suffering, anger, frustration, and mistrust on both sides. It has never resulted in two people experiencing deeper connection, intimacy, or trust. It is a direct violation of the compassion pillar. In fact, snooping is one of the biggest factors I have seen in relationships ending.

Yet, some people, fueled by a sense of insecurity and self-doubt, will continue to violate their partner's boundaries, invade their privacy, and look for something that is none of their business. I'm sure while you've been reading this page dozens of people have poked their noses where they don't belong. And they are next in line to break up, or seek the assistance of a relationship therapist.

Still, if you need further discouragement, here is the scoop on why snooping never works out in the snooper's favor. Snooping results in one or more of the following:

- The snooper doesn't find anything, and continues to live with a lingering fear that their partner is keeping something from them.
- The snooper does find something confusing and is not sure what it means. Then they must figure out whether to consult their findings with an outside friend or family member, who is now involved in the deception.
- The snooper does find something "incriminating" and has to decide what to do about it, which ultimately leaves them with three options:

1. Say nothing and harbor fear and resentment.
2. Again drag that innocent bystander into the violation.
3. Say something and have their partner experience a sense of violation, betrayal, and inability to trust the snooper ever again.

So why do people snoop? Most snoopers would say they are doing it because their partner did something "suspicious." They believe that they will experience a sense of relief if they just knew "the truth." But the real truth is: snooping comes from a fear-based core belief that one is fundamentally unlovable.

For example, Marcy fundamentally thinks of herself as unworthy, unsexy, undeserving of love from Max. So when Max demonstrates interest, affection, and devotion, it is in direct contradiction to the deep beliefs she holds about herself. In order to resolve the tension from this discrepancy, Marcy unconsciously seeks to "prove" that she is truly unworthy.

She snoops through Max's computer knowing that she does not have permission to do so. During this act she feels disgusted with herself, which further proves she is unworthy of another person's pure love. She eventually finds some porn on Max's computer. When Max learns of Marcy's violation, he feels violated, betrayed, and breaks things off. Marcy is alone and further convinced no man can ever love her.

Marcy's actions are an illustration of a "self fulfilling prophesy." She inherently and unconsciously believes she isn't good enough for Max. She does something out of integrity to prove to herself that she's not good enough for Max. Max finds out what she did and breaks if off, which "proves" to Marcy she isn't good enough.

When someone snoops they are searching for a way to sabotage their relationship with another, thereby confirming the "prophesy" that they were never worthy to begin with. If you choose to participate in a Rational Relationship, then you will make decisions that promote compassion, not betrayal. Remember, "compassion" simply means that you act and react from a basic level of caring for yourself and in integrity with others. If you claim to respect your partner, you don't knowingly hurt them by invading their privacy. If you say you want to increase trust in your relationship, then you don't act in an untrustworthy manner.

So what do you do if you have a valid concern about your partner's honesty? *Ask them.* Use the communication tools in Chapter Five to facilitate an honest and compassionate discussion about your concern. And if you don't believe them after that? Then explore what you are doing with your integrity if you engaging in a relationship with someone you can't trust. Is it them, or is it you?

Focus on creating a relationship that is grounded in integrity and leave out the pain-inflicting act of snooping. Find more honorable and effective ways to communicate your fears and doubts. If you are living consistently in your integrity, then you will find it much easier to trust yourself and others, and be less likely to sabotage your relationship.

Rational Compassion Exercises

These are tools and ideas that I have used to increase the Compassion Pillar with couples in my practice. I encourage you not simply to read them as ideas: do consider implementing these actions as ways to enhance compassion and intimacy in your own relationship(s).

Give Presents Of Presence—Set aside a time during the week in which the two of you are together with phones put away, computers shut down, televisions turned off, where you just focus on the other. One person talks (using the Rational Communication strategies from the previous chapter), and the other listens. Eye contact is made consistently during this exchange. Each is allowed to ask clarifying questions, including, "What do you prefer from me right now, just to listen, or to help with the problem?" Then you take turns and allow the other person to speak. Although there are no absolutes, it is recommended that the first time you do this, to plan 30 minutes (each person gets 15 minutes). At the end, check in with each other and ask how it felt to do this exercise. It's perfectly acceptable to talk about how weird it feels to do it, but you can also talk about what you liked about it, and how it felt for you to spend a full 30 minutes of present time with your partner.

Freaky Friday Exercise—In order to increase empathy in couples, I will often employ the "Freaky Friday" technique which has each person "magically" become the other, and answer questions accordingly. If they don't know the answer, then they can either guess, or say, "I don't remember," and move on. Not knowing an answer means they have something more to talk about the during the Presence exercise above.

Using Glenn and Maria from the previous Communication chapter, I would approach the exercise this way:

"As of this moment, magic dust has descended upon the room, and you have now suddenly switched bodies. You must spend the next 30 minutes inside the body of your partner and answer questions for them accordingly."

I turn to Glenn and ask:
"Maria, I will start with you first:
What is your favorite food?
What is your favorite music?
Who is your favorite person to talk to at work?
Who is your least favorite person at work?
What have been your biggest challenges learning English as a second language?
What challenges do you regularly face as a Latina?
What excites you the most about having this baby?
What scares you the most about having this baby?
What excites you the most about marrying Glenn?
What scares you the most about marrying Glenn?"

I then turn to Maria and ask:
"Okay Glenn, you are next:
What is your favorite food?
What is your favorite music?
What are you most looking forward to in your new job?
What are you most dreading about your new job?
How have you dealt with disappointments in your career?

What would you say has been the biggest obstacle you have overcome in your life?
What excites you the most about having this baby?
What scares you the most about having this baby?
What excites you the most about marrying Maria?
What scares you the most about marrying Maria?"

I have added or subtracted questions at various points. Regardless of what is asked, the intended outcome is for both members to gain a here-and-now experience of what it's like to experience life from the other's perspective. This exercise frequently deepens and enriches appreciation and compassion between two people.

The Morose Impermanence Exercise—This exercise is intended to increase awareness of the impermanence of life so that couples are reminded not to take anything for granted on any given day. I do not use this exercise with everyone, but will consider employing it when couples are engaging in a viscous cycle of attack-blame dynamics with the assumption they have plenty of time to work things through.

This simply consists of asking each person a basic question: If you knew your partner was going to die tomorrow, what would say to them today?

Morose, yes. Irrational, no. Living in New York has allowed me vast opportunities to work with people who were directly impacted by the events on 9/11/01, and who will never take a single day with a loved one for granted again. Similarly, the increase of mass shootings and violent actions in the U.S. remind us to hold our loved ones tight, as we never can be sure what tomorrow will bring.

Knowing that life is impermanent, why waste one second holding back on telling your partner how you feel? Why take one single day for granted? Exploring these questions illuminates the reality of impermanence and gives you an impetus to change your perspective on your relationship's problems. It can add compassion, meaning, and depth to every conversation from that moment on.

These exercises really helped in working with newlyweds, Marti and Brian, who came in after experiencing a "disastrous" honeymoon in Italy.

"I just couldn't believe it," Marti began, "I've waited all my life to go Italy, then all he wants to do is lay around the hotel. Every day there were hikes, tours, museums, drives. And he just wanted to hang out."

"That is a complete exaggeration," Brian shot back. "There were plenty of things I was willing to do. But for God's sake, this was our honeymoon, not boot camp. We didn't have to wake up at the crack of dawn every day to do a million things. I like my vacations to be more leisurely, relaxing. I like to get a lot of sleep, take my time, and do non-touristy things."

"And I like to see as much as possible, do as much as possible. I may never get to see Italy again in my life. I didn't want to miss one second of anything."

With this information, I proposed my Freaky Friday exercise, took out my magic wand, and started asking Brian questions as "Marti."

(To Brian) "Marti, what does going to Italy mean to you?"

Brian, as Marti, replied, "It's a chance to see something I've never seen before…(pause) my family didn't have much money growing up, we didn't get to travel and see the world like other families. I've always wanted to see different places but never thought I could. So this honeymoon seemed like a once-in-a-lifetime opportunity that I wanted to take full advantage of."

Marti smiled and became tearful as Brian spoke from her point of view. She nodded to him and grabbed his hand, acknowledging he was understanding her in a way most did not.

I then turned to Marti, "So tell me Brian, what did the trip to Italy mean to you?"

Marti, as Brian, replied, "It was an opportunity to slow down. I work pretty hard in that job I don't love so much. This was a chance for me to slow down and spend quality time with my beautiful new bride. And it was going great until she nagged me to death. I would have had a lot more fun with her if she just could have chilled out."

As we continued the questions, both Brian and Marti expressed insights into each other's experience and a willingness to learn more. They both expressed a level of empathy and compassion that enabled them to leave Italy behind and plan their next trip, this time to Greece. This time they agreed to think ahead, and decided it was perfectly fine for Marti to go off on her own and explore without any resentments or judgments against Brian.

They continued to use the Freaky Friday exercise on their own, and incorporated a portion of it into their Presents of Presence exercise on a consistent basis. Within months they discontinued therapy with me, happily noting they were doing well maintaining the "pillars" on their own, knowing that they could always return to treatment if the pillars needed extra "reinforcing" in the future.

Biggest Obstacle to Compassion: Anger/Pain

Let's face it. When you are angry with your partner, it can be pretty hard to see straight, much less feel a sense of compassion. In a country where "forgiveness" is rarely spoken of in high regard, most Americans tend to go for the ol' "eye for an eye, tooth for a tooth" path of reaction. Of course, when you are in pain, the most natural thing is to want to get back at the person you perceive caused it. However, acting out on these feelings can be the worst mistake you can make for your relationship.

First, let's acknowledge what anger truly is: a reaction to feeling pain that leads to suffering. As discussed in the previous chapter, "pain" is an automatic physical or emotional response to something that happens. Your partner does something that hurts you, and you experience pain. Then your mind starts revving up by saying, "That should not have happened, he should not have done that, he won't get away with it..." and voila, you have a recipe for "suffering," which in this example takes the form of anger. Now your brain starts to recall the evidence of previous wrongs, formulates revenge plots, fantasizes about making him suffer, and righting the wrong in the name of all that is good and decent in this world.

It is very difficult to maintain a compassionate stance toward the other person in these moments. Sometimes you just can't get there, and that is perfectly fine. What is not acceptable in the context of Rational Relating is to take action based on that intense emotion. "Action" may include impulsively breaking up, using hate speech, keying their car, hacking their computer, spreading lies or private information about them, gossiping to family members, and even violent behavior. These types of reactions are the opposite of "compassionate" and can do permanent damage to a pillar, as well as your own freedom.

What *is* okay in the context of a Rational Relationship is to ask for a time out, some space, a separation, and even a couple's session. Use the anger as an opportunity to learn something new about yourself. Acknowledge that behind all anger is a profound sense of pain and hurt. Like a Tootsie Pop, anger is the hard crusted coating that protects the fragile (vulnerable) candy inside. It may seem strange to compare pain to something sugary and sweet, but the hurt truly can be a gift when it helps you grow and evolve. If you can perceive your hurt in this way, it just might help you work through it with minimal suffering, and more understanding for yourself and others.

Use the anger as an opportunity to learn something new about yourself.

Finding compassion for a partner in the midst of emotional turmoil does not mean that staying in a relationship with them is always the best option. There may be practical reasons why you choose not to return, including concerns for your physical safety. Even in this scenario, however, it still can benefit you to carry compassion as an ultimate goal. If you choose to work in that direction, here are some tips to assist:

1. **No one is all good or all bad**. Most are basically good people who mess up from time to time. If you love them now, or if you ever did, then there must be good somewhere in them. Try to see that now.

2. **Everyone is doing the best they can given the set of tools they have been given on this earth.** There are always logical explanations for why people do the things they do. You may not like or agree with those explanations, but they exist nonetheless.

3. **Everyone manifests pain differently.** Some adults channel pain from early in life in ways that are cruel and abusive to others, and absent of compassion. *You* may not be able to remain compassionate toward all others when you are intensely hurt and angry. The same is true for everyone else.

4. **Regaining compassion ultimately benefits you more than anyone else.** Being able to see someone's humanity and value through their harmful actions can allow you to experience a sense of deeper connection and faith in other humans. This ability will help you as you move forward in this or other relationships.

When Nice Hurts

Being nice at the cost of being honest is a huge violation of compassion, and can do severe damage to a relationship's structure. You may think you doing the right thing by sparing someone's feelings. But in the long run, withholding information and feelings ends up hurting the person you care about. How does that work?

At the conclusion of a first date, one person says, "I had a great time, I'll call you," when he really means, "God get me out of here, I'm never doing this again." If the other person really did have a great time, then he or she will likely be checking their phone and email, waiting for the call or message that doesn't come, and experiencing anxiety, hurt, and pain when it doesn't happen. The compassionate option would have been to demonstrate integrity and communicate effectively early on.

Another destructively "nice" example frequently takes place in longer term relationships when one person develops resentment against the other. I have seen many husbands and wives who are all smiles to their spouses, then roll their eyes and mutter something sarcastic and diminishing about their spouse under their breath when their supposed beloveds aren't listening. The appearance will look nice, while under the surface there is palpable sense of tension and anger.

And of course we all know what happens when "nice" women fake orgasms. It is usually done from an initial position of trying to reduce their partner's insecurities and fears. Yet if (and when) the man ever finds out, it can do irreparable damage to his sense of trust and ability to enjoy pleasure and intimacy with his partner.

There are times that being polite, considerate, and thoughtful of another person's feelings helps to make your relationship strong. A simple, "You look great today," or a gentle, "Please don't forget to pick up the kids after their soccer game" can go a long way toward promoting connection, respect, and the feeling you are on the same team. Consideration and respect for another's person feelings is an important ingredient in any satisfying long-term relationship.

But being nice merely for appearance's sake also work against the relationship if it's used to cover up painful feelings, withhold important information, harbor passive-aggressive anger, or purposely deceive your partner. Here are some guidelines for avoiding the pitfalls of cruel "nice."

1. **Practice the Golden Rule of Do Unto Others.** Don't treat your partner the way you wouldn't want to be treated. If you don't want your partner to lie to you about sex, don't fake orgasms. If you want your partner to treat you well, don't smile while stifling disgust.

2. **Communicate Effectively.** Use your words to effectively and sincerely express your hopes, desire and intentions. Learn ways of compassionately saying "no" in order to live more fully in integrity. Chapter Four offered tools for increasing integrity in your interactions.

3. **Accept That You Don't Control What Others Feel.** Being honest instead of nice means someone's feelings might get hurt. It will do your relationship less damage if feelings get hurt earlier than later. If you're not interested in that person, say so. If you're not having orgasms, say so. You don't get to control how people react to your

words, but you do get a say in whether you are going to interact with yourself and with others with compassion.

4. **Understand the difference between "nice" and "compassionate."** Nice is how people act and react to each other in situations. Compassion is a grounded stance of caring for humanity, and seeking to do no intentional harm. It may not be considered "nice" to tell someone you are no longer interested in seeing them romantically, but it is compassionate to let them know the relationship isn't going any further so they can move forward.

Sara and Bradley on Compassion

Bradley (B): Okay, fine, so we are getting along better now. But that doesn't mean we're still not having real problems. Sara is holding this wedding over me like a toxic oil spill. Can we just get that settled once and for all?

Damon (D): I think that's a great idea. Before we settle that, I'd like to return to the Relationship Inventory of Values list we did earlier. Sara, you listed Compassion fairly high on your list, and so did Bradley. What does "compassion" mean to you?

Sara (S): Well, like it says on there, you act on concern for others. You treat others the way you want to be treated, maybe sometimes better than you want to be treated.

D: Is it compassionate, by that definition, for a wife to mock her husband's penis, or any physical attribute?

S: No, it definitely is not, and I feel really horrible I threw that out during our first session. (To Bradley) I am really sorry I said that.

B: Thank you for apologizing for that.

D: And it makes sense that you both know the exact thing to say that will hurt the feelings of the other. That is what empathy is really all about. But I ask you each to consider if you are being compassionate in those moments. And Bradley, I recall certain remarks you made about Sara's nose that were less than compassionate.

B: It's true, I did say that because I knew it would hurt you. That's not right. I'm sorry.

S: It did hurt me, and thank you for apologizing.

D: Now that we have a better comprehension of what compassion looks like, and what it doesn't look like, I want to ask Sara, is it compassionate to put someone in a situation where they will knowingly suffer ridicule and discomfort?

S: (Pause), No, it isn't. Look, my family doesn't mean to be cruel, that's just the way they are. But I can see how someone would feel that way around them, I can see why Bradley would be uncomfortable with that.

D: Okay, so it appears that you would be out of your integrity by forcing Bradley to do something that would upset and distress him.

S: Alright, I will agree with that. I'm sad, I'm really disappointed. And to be honest, I'm pissed off. But you are right, it would be outside my integrity to knowingly put Bradley in a position where he will be suffering.

B: Thank you. Thank you for that, I mean it. So it's okay if I don't go?

S: It's not okay, but it's okay. Do you know what I mean? I may not be okay with it, but I can get over it.

D: Now Bradley, you also placed Compassion rather high on your list of priorities, even higher than Sara's. What does that mean to you?

B: Well, I thought it meant that I gave her things she wanted that I thought would make her happy. Now I'm not so sure.

D: Sara, how can Bradley demonstrate more compassion for you?

S: He can stop calling my family names. I know they're crazy, but your name calling doesn't help any. They're my family, they are a part of me, I love them.

B: Done. I give you my word, I will not call them names anymore.

D: How does that feel to hear Bradley say that, Sara?

S: It's good, but...I'm still struggling with this. Maybe it's not "rational" but I still think a husband should come to his wife's sister's wedding.

D: Okay, will you let me ask you this? God forbid, what if something happened to Bradley tomorrow? And this was the last night on earth you could spend with him. How would you spend it?

S: That's a horrible question.

D: Why is it horrible?

S: Because you're asking me to conceive of something horrible, something tragic, something I hope would never happen!

D: Why not?

S: Because I love him so much! I love him in our home, in our bed, even on the couch. I can't imagine any kind of life without him, I don't want to imagine any kind of life without him.

D: And how important is the wedding right now?

S: It's not. I don't care about the friggin' wedding, I just don't want to lose him.

B: It's okay, you're not going to lose me.

S: I do love you, I do.

B: (Quietly) I know.

D: So right now, I think you are both experiencing is a heightening of emotions that happens when we are confronted with the reality of impermanence. I agree it would be horrible for anything to happen to either one of you. But eventually something will happen to every one of us. For whatever time you two have, do you want to spend it focused on the things the other person did "wrong," or do you want to spend it appreciative of the other person's life, in gratitude they are still here?

S: Gratitude is working pretty well for me right now.

B: Definitely. Me, too.

In this example I drew upon their stated values from the Relationship Inventory of Values list, and helped both to see how compassion was or was not consistent with their actions. Even when Sara agreed to be "rational" about the wedding, she still experienced suffering based on her thought, "a husband should go with his wife to her sister's wedding." Using the Morose Impermanence Exercise, I was able to help Sara shift her emotions from resentment to gratitude. Ideally, she will get more in the habit of doing this on her own, and not require Bradley or me to remind her of this. By using such tools, both Sarah and Bradley increased compassion and appreciation for the other and took one more significant step toward reinforcing their relationship's pillars.

The Rational Relating Compassion Scale

Compassion can best be described as a way of acknowledging and witnessing the core self within others humans, and then making your best effort not to inflict deliberate suffering on those people around you. It can be expressed as an action, a thought pattern, and an essential pillar of Rational Relationships. The scale below offers you an idea of how strong your relationship's Compassion Pillar is today. Circle the number that corresponds best to your current relationship:

1. There is no consideration or thought given to the other person's feelings during the process of communication and problem solving. One or both partners simply "do their thing" without considering the welfare of the other.

2. There is some ability to demonstrate caring and support for the other partner, but with no concerted effort or consistency in actions.

3. There are some inconsistent and unpredictable expressions of genuine empathy, consideration, patience and presence, but they can not be relied upon, and/or might be limited to specific situations.

4. There is a general sense of empathy and concern for the other's core humanity in most situations, with a few exceptions. There may have been a significant action taken against the other in the past year (i.e., one person violated the agreement, intentionally caused pain, knowingly used hurtful language).

5. There is genuine respect/empathy consistently conveyed for each partner in all contexts. No intentional actions/words used against another in past year. Any incidental behaviors are sincerely apologized for.

CHAPTER SEVEN

The Responsibility Pillar

Most of us have learned that if we are feeling bad, sad, or just generally irritable, it has to be someone or something else's fault. We have all been conditioned to blame a partner or spouse, a family member, a boss, a stranger in traffic, Wall Street, Congress, or even the weather for our mood. This belief has been reinforced in politics, entertainment, and even by psychotherapists who ask, "How did that make you feel?"

The truth is no one has the power to make you suffer. Ask yourself if you have recently said any of the following:

_____ makes me upset.
_____ hurt my feelings.
_____ is stressing me out!

Now take a look at what is inherent in these words: Blame and power are assigned to people or things outside of yourself. If you allow someone else's behavior to determine how you feel, then you're going to be pretty stressed out, frustrated, depressed, resentful, and a whole host of unpleasant experiences.

I am completely aware that this goes against the grain of what many learn about relationships. You probably learned early in life that your feelings and moods are based on what other people say and do, and on outside situations. You have come to believe it is your job in life to find effective ways to control those people and situations so you can minimize or avoid experiencing negative feelings. Partners and spouses, then, become a means to an end instead of an end in themselves. Or to put it another way, loved ones in relationships remain in your good graces when they are "making" you have the feelings you want. When they no longer are performing their duties to make you feel good, you experience disappointment, hopelessness, frustration, and then come to therapy blaming those rat bastards for not doing their job!

The truth is no one has the power to make you suffer.

Traditional models of psychotherapy support the notion that one must effectively search for blame outside of themselves when coping with depression and disturbance. Inevitably the beginning of this search starts with one's mother, thereby setting up a structure of institutional misogyny in which women are responsible for the "neuroses" of the world. (Where are the fathers in this equation? Good luck getting an answer to that!). When a therapists ask, "How does that make you feel," they are effectively reinforcing the idea that your feelings are decided by other people, places, things. It is a passive encouragement of victimization that serves no role in promoting mental health or wellness.

When I was younger, I did believe it was other people's fault when I felt bad. I blamed my brother, parents, teachers, authority figures, coworkers, and friends if I wasn't happy. I would be revved up for any conflict, battle, protest, petition, or ready to stop traffic on the highway, if it meant I could blame anyone else for my own inner sense of misery and self-hatred.

In my early 30s I came to realize that this was a stale and powerless stance. I read Victor Frankl's *Man's Search For Meaning*, which described how a concentration camp survivor could take responsibility for finding meaning even in the most painful of circumstances. I studied how Tina Turner and Nelson Mandela survived extremely abusive and oppressive circumstances only to recognize how true liberation takes place in the mind first, situation second. In recent years I learned about the work of Eva Kor, who also is a concentration camp survivor, and speaks out on the liberation of forgiveness. If they can be completely responsible for their emotional health, then maybe I am completely responsible when I get annoyed with someone in traffic.

In Rational Relating, the purpose of your relationship is not to fill an emotional void. Connections are created to increase what you already have inside of you. Relationships serve to enhance and increase the abundance of beauty, power, and magnificence that you already possess. You may have been taught to believe that these qualities are outside of you, and that you must get them from someone else. If so, then that is the worst lie you have ever been told.

We are all born into this world as perfect, amazing, and resilient creatures. Babies don't need to be told how great they are, they already know it is their birthright. It is soon afterward that children start getting the memo: You are not _____ [smart, thin, attractive, valuable, worthy, important, lovable] enough as you are. Oftentimes children start learning this from family members, and if not, then from other children and teachers in school. If they are lucky enough to escape the negative programming from these sources, they will inevitably get the message from movies, television, or magazines.

Very few children are taught how to resist such oppressive and overwhelming messages. But make no mistake: Children have an easier time understanding these concepts than most adults. When given adequate and appropriate information, kids are very capable of resisting punitive shameful messages and learning how to say (and mean), "No one has the right to make me feel bad about myself." When I am asked by adults, "How do I learn to love myself?" I always reply, "You don't need to learn how to love yourself, you need how to unlearn all the information that has gotten in the way of you loving yourself." Children have much less unlearning to do, and are more able to readily access that newborn spirit that knew she was perfect to begin with.

Sadly, most children grow up without this information, and become adults who intrinsically carry a sense of guilt and insecurity, with a fundamental baseline of self-doubt. When they meet a potential partner who distracts them from these painful feelings, they experience that person with ecstatic relief, and mistake the diversion for "falling in love." That new partner, then, only serves a purpose if they are providing that sense of distraction and comfort. In reality, no other human can consistently sustain this task and continuously feed someone the emotional nutrients that they won't feed themselves. Couples then get disappointed, get angry, go through breakups and divorces, only to repeat the cycle again with the next potential candidate.

There is a silver lining to this admittedly grim view of "romance." You need not ever engage in this cruel heartbreaking spiral if you simply stop looking for emotional answers outside of yourself and start getting back in touch with the love, joy, and ecstasy that were your birthright from day one. There is positively no reason to continue the search for something that doesn't exist. You have the answers, you have the power, you have the key, no one else.

Relationships serve to enhance and increase the abundance of beauty, power, and magnificence that you already possess.

Once you take full responsibility for that self-love, relationships are dessert. They become an instrument of expression for the savory magnificence that you already are. You are able to recognize the sweet beauty in others, and give and receive authentic love with others.

All of this begins by consciously and rationally taking full responsibility for your emotional, physical, and spiritual experience. The following offers several ideas and tools on how to accomplish this.

The Rational Responsibility Checklist:

- Remind yourself constantly of the fundamental principle of Rational Emotive Behavioral Therapy (REBT): People are not upset by other people's behavior, they are upset by what they tell themselves about other people's behavior. Write this on a post-it and put it up where you'll see it (bathroom mirror, refrigerator, dashboard, etc.).
- Make a list when you first wake up of at least five things you are grateful for.
- Stop using language and conversation to blame others for how you are feeling.

- Surround yourself with people who are also seeking to take responsibility for their experience and who will support you in this process.
- Protect yourself from being verbally abused by others.
- Do not engage in social media with individuals who are trying to harm you.
- In any given situation decide how you want to feel before you enter, and then stick to it!
- Do not expose yourself to the bullying and fear mongering of television "news" shows that seek to scare you instead of empowering you.
- Read books and blogs written by people who have survived adversity and have something to teach you about resiliency and strength in this world.
- Journal every day to take a stock of your thoughts and feelings, and see where you can apply rational thinking to situations (and there is always more work to be done in this process).

The Feeling Fraction Exercise

This exercise is intended to demonstrate the logical system of feelings, and to illustrate how you can take full responsibility for your moods at any time. It is called "The Feeling Fraction" because just like mathematics, your heart abides by certain rhythms and patterns; it's simply a matter of becoming aware of them.

In mathematics you begin with a simple equation:

$$\frac{2}{4} = \frac{?}{10}$$

Using a logical sequence of rational thinking, you can see that "2" is to "4" in the first equation, as the number "5" would be to "10" in the second equation. Now let's see how this can apply to rational thinking:

Thought	I'm no good, I'm a bad person	???
Feeling	Depressed, low self-worth	Content, high self-worth

What do you imagine the thoughts might be that go into the box with the questions marks? There could be many, but most likely they would say something like, "I'm a good person, I help others, I am smart, attractive, I have intrinsic value," or something along those lines. By consciously and methodically changing your thoughts you automatically have more access to the result of feeling more content and enjoying higher self-worth. Let's try another:

Thought	Nothing is as it used to be, everything is falling apart in society	???
Feeling	Angry, frustrated, irritable	Serene, peaceful, accepting

What are the thoughts that would lead to the desired result of feeling more serene, peaceful, and accepting? Again, there could be a number of them, but they would probably resemble something like, "Things are actually going pretty well, change is inevitable and often a good thing." What the Feeling Fraction points out is that how you feel is your choice, and your responsibility.

"But moods are not math," you may be thinking. "Changing the way I feel is much more complicated than this." Actually, *it is this simple.* I didn't say it was easy, I just said it was simple. No matter how your psychological, spiritual, religious, medical, chemical, or biological theory explains emotional experience, the one thing that remains constant is the idea that one must change their mind in order to change their mood.

Even the most traditional Freudian would have to concede that it's not "insight" that produces change, it is what you do with that insight. You can spend years on the analyst's couch figuring out how your mother/father/dead dog impact your ability to be in a happy relationship but it won't help a bit until you *decide* to change.

Similarly, all religious and spiritual practices involve some sort of practice in the mind. Whether that involves meditating, praying, confessing, or singing, it involves accessing serenity or nirvana by aligning your thoughts in some form with a Higher Power.

The most staunch clinical doctor who advocates for the use of psychotropic medications to treat mood "disorders" can look at their own files to see that taking a pill, in the absence of any cognitive changes, is usually futile. If you are taking an antidepressant to feel better, while continuously and actively thinking thoughts about what a horrible person you are, that pill isn't going to have the chance to do much good. Doctors also know that someone with a terminal or chronic disease is often able to have longer periods of serenity and happiness when they are focused on positive thoughts.

Any way you slice it, the way we think is the primary motivator for how we feel. Why not cut to the chase by figuring out what you want to feel *first*, and then change your thoughts accordingly?

"But moods are not math," you may be thinking. **"Changing the way I feel is much more complicated than this."** Actually, *it is this simple.*

So how does this apply to Rational Relating? The example given by Kevin and Liz will help illustrate. They have been coming to therapy for several months and consistently complain about the other's thoughts, mood swings, and behaviors. Liz is a school teacher who devotes much of her time to school. Kevin is a construction worker who has been out of work on disability due to an injury at his work site six months ago. They state they have been constantly bickering, beginning with Kevin being upset that she works such long hours, and her resentment that Kevin is "stressing me out."

I used the Feeling Fraction exercise, starting with Liz. The first step was asking her how she felt, and she named the feelings in the lower left corner. Then I asked what she was thinking as she was experiencing these feelings, and she named the thoughts in the upper left corner. Finally, I asked her how she *wants* to feel, and she named the emotions in the lower right corner:

Thought	Kevin should be more independent. He should learn how to handle his depression and deal with his problems. If he took better care of himself I wouldn't be so stressed and exhausted all the time.	???
Feeling	Resentful, bitter, frustrated	Calm, acceptance, loving

Based on this equation, I asked Liz what thoughts she could imagine that would result in the experience of having more calm, acceptance, and loving feelings toward Kevin. She thought quite a bit about it, and came up with some ideas based on our work together in previous months.

"I would put in the blank box: 'There are no shoulds. He's doing the best he can. He's not choosing to be in pain, he didn't ask for that accident to happen. He's lonely sometimes, he's scared. I could be more patient if I set my mind to it. It's not Kevin's fault if I'm stressed and exhausted, a lot of that has to do with my work and not setting boundaries in some situations at the school.'"

I asked Liz if those thoughts were resulting in the preferred feelings of "calm, acceptance, and loving."

"They help. It's not perfect, but refocusing my thoughts helps me to have more access to those feelings."

Then I asked Kevin to do the same exercise. This is what his Feeling Fraction looked like:

Thought	She works so damn hard all the time. They completely take advantage of her there, and she lets them. I wish she was home more often. It's like she would rather be anywhere with anyone than at home with me.	???
Feeling	Angry, sad, frustrated	Worthwhile, important, valuable

So looking over Kevin's Feeling Fraction, I began to explore what thoughts could possibly go in the empty box. He struggled with this, because describing feelings and thoughts did not come instinctively to Kevin. He was raised that men "don't do these things," and that Liz "should just know certain things." However, the idea that the way he experienced life was in his control did appeal to him, and was consistent with his concept of masculinity.

Based on this, Kevin worked toward finding thoughts to fill in the empty box. He ultimately was able to share, "My worth is not based on Liz being home. My problems now are mainly with my physical limitations, not with Liz. Yes, they take advantage of her, but she loves the work she does there, and I like that she has a job that makes her happy." Despite these words helping Kevin to feel "better," he was still a long way from feeling the worth, importance, and value that he sought in the lower right box. I asked Liz if she thought she could contribute some ideas.

"Your very existence is worthwhile and important to me," she said to Kevin. "Don't you know, you make my life so meaningful. I can go to work and tolerate the madness there because I know I get to see you at the end of the day. Your body may be going through changes, but you still light up the lives of so many people besides me. Your family, your friends, all feel better when you are in the room. If that's not valuable, I don't know what is."

Kevin smiled and nearly looked tearful as she said these words. I asked Kevin if he could repeat her message back in a way that could help him feel worthwhile, important, and valuable, even when she wasn't home.

"Okay. I can't do the things I used to do, and that has been making me depressed. But there are many things I still can do, there are still many ways I am valuable and worthwhile to Liz and others. That definitely feels closer."

By writing down their Feeling Fractions, both Liz and Kevin were not only able to take responsibility for their own emotions, but to draw strength and empowerment from the other as well. This promoted a sense of connection as opposed to completion. Both members learned the hard way that they can not depend on the other to meet their emotional needs. They did learn, however, that they can work together to create a connection that expanded and enhanced the feelings they wanted to experience. Over time they continued to work on The Feeling Fractions together, and supported each other in effectively and responsibly managing their daily moods.

To Forgive Or Not To Forgive?

Without a clear and rational approach to forgiveness, relationship pillars can remain weakened and vulnerable. How can you move forward in a relationship after your partner said or did something hurtful to you?

Let's begin by clearly stating what forgiveness is not. Forgiveness is not an agreement that the other person's action is acceptable. It is not indicating that there is approval of one's decisions, or that the violation will be forgotten. It is not expressing that trust will automatically rebuild, and it is not a validation that it is okay for that person to do the same thing again.

What forgiveness does is restore you as the authority of your affective experience. It allows you to resume full responsibility for how you perceive your partner's behaviors and your reactions. In short, it is your key to empowerment by reclaiming your feelings, moods, and perceptions.

When you approach forgiveness, you simply look at your partner's actions through the lens of, "He was doing the best he could at the time with the tools he was given." If he acted outside of his integrity, then you recognize the role that fear played in driving his behavior. If he acted with integrity, then try to understand what values led to his decision (even if you don't agree with them).

Forgiveness is first and foremost a decision rather than an action. It is a confirmation that all humans, including yourself, are capable of making mistakes. It is a choice of recognizing that most people in this culture are taught to act and react from fear, and that cruelty and insensitivity are oftentimes a direct byproduct of that fear. If you wish to be a catalyst for change, and live in a world with less fear, cruelty, and insensitivity, then it is up to you to stop perpetuating these practices and stop reacting to them in your interpersonal relationships.

This may or may not mean that you *do* something about it. There are situations where the person you are forgiving might be dead, unavailable, or unsafe. You still can make the decision of forgiveness, with or without the other person's involvement.

The consequences of not forgiving others in relationships are twofold. You will either harbor resentment, anger, bitterness, and aggression toward the person you are angry with. Or, you will leave the relationship, and carry all the anger and resentment into your next relationship, thereby "poisoning the well" before the new person even gets a chance. Either way, forgiveness is about taking care of *you* and prioritizing your emotional health in any interaction.

"But how do I do this," I often hear. "That person really hurt me in ways I can't get over." Forgiveness is not about getting over anything. It is about getting *through* the pain and betrayal. Here are tips for beginning the process:

1. Recognize the person who hurt you was reacting to some form of fear or pain of their own.
2. Understand that most people react to fear and pain by hurting others, intentionally or unintentionally.
3. Forgive your participation in the hurtful event, no matter how big or small.
4. Choose to be a catalyst for ending the cycle of fear and pain by not striking back at the person, or intentionally hurting anyone else.
5. Accept that your pain is not going to go away immediately. But when you forgive you start to create a possibility for pain to be transformed into strength and resilience.

6. Remember, forgiveness is a decision, not an action. You may decide to forgive your partner and still choose to leave the relationship. Or you may forgive your partner and choose to work it through. Either way your peace and joy are your responsibility, and your decision.

Biggest Obstacle to Responsibility: Empowerment

Why would someone not want to take responsibility for their emotional well being? Why would they prefer to assign blame to a partner? Because for many people the idea of being fully empowered to manage their feelings and moods is outside the acceptability of their comfort zone.

Remember, you are told from birth to perceive your feelings outside of yourself. You are consistently conditioned to believe that any sense of upset, sadness, frustration, or stress is from something or someone "out there," and similarly, so is any sense of happiness, tranquility, self-worth, or value. As mentioned earlier, nearly all women and men in this culture are taught that "romance" means that someone "makes" you feel more of the good stuff you want to feel, and less of the bad junk you do not.

If you could truly accept and embrace full responsibility for your feelings, you would have more strength and empowerment available to you than ever before. You could have access to levels of acceptance and serenity that may seem unimaginable right now. Relationships would be avenues to sharing authentic joy versus the roller coaster of false highs and lows. It would be positively revolutionary!

Yet like most revolutions and changes in thinking, this level of empowerment would be resisted by many. After all, what would happen to plastic surgeons if women and men realized they are simply beautiful as they are, and created relationships with others that nurtured their sense of true inner value? What would happen to the pharmaceutical companies if people realized they could manage their moods and maintain emotional satisfaction without a pill? Heck, what would us wonderful Marriage and Family Therapists do if all of you decided to have blissful fulfilling relationships without us? I may have to go back to waiting tables!

For many people the idea of being fully empowered to manage their feelings and moods is outside the acceptability of their comfort zone.

As you can see, the barriers to your experience of empowerment are quite large from the inside and the outside, and this is why people often choose not to take responsibility for their mental and spiritual wellness. It does not mean that you have to surrender and give it up. Using the ideas in this book consistently, you and your loved ones will have the tools and skills to practice Rational Responsibility in a way that maintains empowerment and enhances connection. The choice is yours.

(And for the record, I'd be fine waiting tables again if it meant that people in the world were so healed and happy that they no longer required the services of therapists!).

Your Single Responsibility

There is an unquestioned assumption in U.S. culture that you are better off married. This gets manifested in movies that promote romance and marriage, tax laws that give married partners breaks, medical insurance that offers married couples benefits, religious rituals that include two people, political activism that focuses on marriage as the ultimate goal of a relationship, not to mention your well-intentioned family members who look at you with sympathy asking, "Are you dating anyone?" This pressure can lead to people feeling inadequate or incomplete if they are not in a relationship, and can put on a significant strain on the dating process if one person is on the hunt for a husband or wife.

The truth is, there are times in your life when you may choose not to engage in a serious relationship with another person. You might be focused on completing your education, building your career, traveling the world, or experiencing a series of adventures that a primary partner would eclipse.

It is perfectly rational and acceptable to choose not to be in a primary relationship with another person. You may want to embrace the unencumbered freedom of living where you want, socializing with friends, staying out all night, working long hours, eating what you want, all without the consultation or approval of another. Single life for you might be perfectly satisfying and content, and that is great.

What is not rational and acceptable is when someone who wants to be single pretends they don't want to be, or succumbs to the aforementioned pressures of being in a relationship because they "should." Or to put it another way, it *is* your responsibility to communicate if you prefer to be single. Instead of making excuses and saying it's other people's "fault," or that you can't find the "right person," just admit you don't want a significant other, and move forward from there.

If being unpartnered is right for you at this time in your life, embrace it! Ignore the social pressures that are set up to shame and condemn you, and embrace the opportunities singlehood can offer. But don't lie about this, or blame others for your choices. Enjoy your single life with integrity and responsibility!

Sara and Bradley on Responsibility

Sara (S): Okay, I can accept Bradley not going to my sister's wedding, I absolutely want to be compassionate about this, and I do appreciate every day with him. But at the same time, he is really hurting my feelings. I don't know what I'm going to tell everyone, I don't how I'm going to be able to relax without him there.

Bradley (B): Well, I don't think you would feel any better with me there. It's not like you particularly seem overjoyed to see me when we are together. Even in bed, when I try to touch you and you pull away, do you know how that makes me feel?

Damon (D): So for just a moment, let's try an exercise that might ease up some of this conflict. Bradley, I want you to start by doing a Feeling Fraction with me [I explain the concept to both].

Bradley's Feeling Fraction:

Thought	Sara's not wanting to have sex with me hurts my feelings, makes me feel like a bad person for wanting sex, and less of a man.	???
Feeling	Sad, guilty, stupid	High self-esteem, good, sexually attractive

D: So what can you imagine would go into that thought box that would lead to you feeling high self-esteem, good, and sexually attractive?

Damon L. Jacobs

B: (Pause). I could decide to value who I am regardless of whether she wants to have sex with me or not. I could say I'm an attractive guy, and a good person no matter what. I'm not perfect, but I have some great qualities regardless.

D: Like what?

B: I care about other people, I try to help others, I volunteer at church, I call my mother once a week...

S: And you're a great singer, don't forget that, you really have a great voice.

B: Thank you. Okay, I'm a good singer... and some people think I look hot in my glasses.

D: And how do you feel right now, Bradley?

B: When I say that I feel better, I feel hopeful, I don't feel ashamed of who I am.

D: That is great. And I would assert that is your right and your responsibility to help yourself feel that way outside of this room. It is not Sara's job to "make" you feel anything, it is your job. Does that make sense?

B: It does when you put it like that.

D: Now Sara, let's look at yours.

Sara's Feeling Fraction:

Thought	A man should go with his wife to her sister's wedding. It really sad he doesn't want to go. I'm scared I won't have any fun without him.	???
Feeling	Pissed off, insulted, frustrated.	Comfortable, accepting, embracing of his quirks

D: Okay, so how do you complete the upper box on the right side? How do you gain access to those feelings you say you want to have?

S: When I remember what you always tell us about having no such thing as "should" or "normal." When I use those words it just makes me angry and makes him seem like this awful man. He is not an awful man.

D: That is a very compassionate perspective. What else?

S: Acceptance is a hard one. You know, Bradley has always been an oddball, and I mean that in a good way. It's one of the things I fell in love with.

D: Then what changed?

S: Not him, he's still the same lovable oddball he always was. Somewhere I became less accepting, maybe I thought I could change him after we got married. The truth is I can only change myself, and I probably need to start doing that right now. Yes, I am disappointed he is not going to the wedding, but I know I'll live through it.

D: Can you think of any advantages to Bradley not being there?

B: Sara, if you think about it honestly, I really think you'll have a better time without me. You won't get stuck playing referee between me and your parents. You can relax, party, have a good time with your family, without worrying about me.

S: I am confused between feeling angry about this, and knowing that you are right. But when I think more about what you are saying, I know it makes sense, and I do feel more accepting about the situation.

D: And that's what this is about. Taking responsibility for your feelings may not solve the "problem," but it gives you the tools to solve the problem. It simply shows each of you that your feelings are your own responsibilities, not your spouse's.

Rational Responsibility Checklist

No one has the power to make you suffer unless you give it to them. When each partner in a couple assumes full responsibility for their peace, joy, and satisfaction, then both are empowered to expand and enhance love through that connection. The scale below gives you an idea of how strong your relationship's responsibility pillar is today. Circle the number that corresponds best to your current relationship:

1. There is complete blame of the other person, one or both hold the other accountable for their feelings (Example: consistent use of statements such as "You made me feel..." or "You made me do ....")

2. There is occasional recognition of one's own participation in one's feelings, while still focusing on one's partner primarily as the source of suffering. (Example: I know I could be content if my partner would agree to have a child with me.)

3. There is authentic recognition of responsibility for one's overall wellness while still believing that the other partner gets the ultimate say in their happiness/sadness. (Example: I could decide to be really happy if my partner remembered our anniversary.)

4. There is an overall recognition of one's own participation and ownership of thoughts, beliefs, actions, and feelings, with occasional examples or situations in which the partner is blamed. (Example: one takes responsibility for their peace of mind while negatively judging a partner who doesn't want to go to a family event.)

5. Full commitment from each person meeting their own needs and being responsible for their thoughts, beliefs, actions, and feelings. Appropriately communicating preferences/desires to the other partner. Relationship is used to connect, not to "complete." (Example: It is not my partner who upset me, it is my thoughts about my partner that upset me.)

CHAPTER EIGHT

The Compromise Pillar

Compromise can often be the most challenging element in Rational Relationships. Even when the other four pillars are strong and durable, couples often struggle deeply with making and maintaining compromises. However, the ideas and exercises in this chapter will make the process a lot smoother.

One of the difficulties people have with the concept of compromise is a sense of fear and dread that stems from the automatic thought that "something will be given up," or, "I'm going to lose in this process." There is a sense that making a change or conceding to a partner's request will result in defeat. In truth, it is exactly the opposite.

Compromise is an opportunity to build a new path with someone *as a team*. It allows you to expand your point of view, and evolve beyond a previously established set of rules. It enables you to have empathy for your partner's preferences, and use that perspective to invent a new solution. It provides a context for creating a new way to solve problems that hasn't ever been tried before within your unique union. In short, compromise offers you much more than "winning" an argument ever can.

Because many tend to think in "all-or-nothing" terms, they see conflicts and problems in a "win-or-lose" or "right-or-wrong" perspective. They tend to think that in any negotiation one is triumphant and one is defeated. This narrow approach tends to result in a couple building resentment toward one another, and diminishing their ability to problem-solve creatively.

Compromise offers you much more than "winning" an argument ever can.

As the other four pillars become solidified and strengthened, compromise becomes more of a joint process. When both members accept full responsibility for their wellness, seek to express affection for the other with compassion, and communicate in ways that promote intimacy and respect integrity, then compromise is a natural outcome. Negotiations may still be challenging, but they are successfully accomplished because there is already a context for Rational Relating to occur.

Go to the "B.E.A.C.H." of Rational Compromise

So how does a couple work together to find a Rational Compromise that enhances satisfaction for both parties, and minimizes ruptures of resentment and bitterness to seep in? It can be done if you remember to go to the "B.E.A.C.H. of Rational Compromise." That is, Balance, Experimentation, Advantage, Creativity, and Humility.

Balance: In order to reach a Rational Compromise, a general sense of fairness and balance needs to be established. If one person is always compromising and the other is not, that is not a Rational Relationship, it is codependence. In order for a compromise to assist and promote connection between two people, both must participate in releasing a desired outcome for the greater good of the relationship.

For instance, Holly wanted to take the kids to Disneyland in California for their summer vacation, while her partner Lori wanted the kids to spend more quality time with her aging father in Texas. Given they only have the time and money to take one vacation a year, how did they choose what to do? By making balance the focal point of their compromise, they explored the possibility of including Lori's father on the Disneyland trip. When that proved not to be feasible, Holly conceded that Disneyland will always be there, whereas Lori's elder father may not. They agreed to see Lori's father this year, and made their plans for Disneyland for the following year. This way they could both have the desired outcome, albeit at different times.

If one person is always compromising and the other is not, that is not a Rational Relationship, it is codependence.

In order for a compromise to affirm and strengthen a connection, there has to be a sense of fairness. That doesn't mean each person will always feel like they have gained or sacrificed at exactly the same rate as each partner. It does mean that there is a general sense of justice that exists within the relationship, and both work together mindfully to make sure there is a larger picture give and take that seems balanced for both. To be fair, this is an ever-changing and ever-evolving process in any relationship. But when two people have balance and fairness as their intended value, and then communicate within the integrity of that value, compromise follows with more ease.

Experimentation: Nothing is permanent in this world. For better or for worse, everything will change. All living things have beginnings and endings. Compromises are no different. Even if you feel like you are "giving up" something important, or making a sacrifice that is outside of your comfort zone, it is usually not forever. When decisions can be changed, why not conduct an experiment, or "play with it" and see how they work out?

This idea works well when two people decide to move in together. I generally recommend that one or both keep their other place if it is possible to do so. Some assert that having an "escape nest" makes authentic compromise harder, but I disagree. It makes logistical sense to take care of your physical, emotional, and financial safety as much as you are reasonably able to do so. Moving in with someone is a huge commitment and involves lots of adjustments. Without an "escape nest" you may be more uncomfortable, frightened, and less able stand up for yourself. This can make experimentation in compromises even harder.

Experiments give you the freedom to commit to a new arrangement so you can get the full breadth of how it works. Jeffrey and Angela found this to be helpful when it came to sex. Over time some of the "zing" had left their sex life, and Angela found herself more often to be the initiator, a role she did not relish.

"If I don't initiate, he won't," she said.

"But when she makes the first move it's kind of a turnoff for me," Jeffrey replied.

So for one week they agreed to try to experiment: Jeffrey agreed to initiate sex at least three times. Angela agreed not to initiate at all. Of course Angela could say "no" if she was not in the mood, but the point was that Jeffrey would try. They came back the next week reporting that they felt much closer, but Angela did not like the idea of waiting for Jeffrey to be affectionate.

Subsequently, the next week they agreed to another experiment: Both Angela and Jeffrey agreed to initiate at least twice. The other could decline, but it was recommended that they both make the effort to choose opportune moments. Further sessions focused more on fantasies, preferences, and how using experimentation they could lead to a richer and more fulfilling sex life.

The great thing about an experiment is that it can be changed at any time, and you get to learn a lot about yourself and your partner in the process. Next time you and your partner get stuck, see if there is a midway point at which you can experiment. Like the old adage says, "Don't knock it till you've tried it!" You don't know if you are going to love or hate a new agreement, so why not give an authentic try before you say "no"? Experimentation gives you the freedom to "play" so you can make an informed decision about whether a compromise works for you or not.

Advantage: Many approach compromise with a dreaded sense of, "Uh oh, I'm going to be losing something here." But what most don't realize is that every negotiation puts you at an advantage to learn something new, try something different, and gain new insights that you had not learned before. People in relationships often see places they never would have seen otherwise, see movies they never would have gone to, hear ideas they would not have been exposed to, have adventures they would not have experienced, and so on.

"Advantage" is defined here as a condition or circumstance that puts one in a favorable or improved position. Not getting what you want in a disagreement may not appear to be favorable to you initially. Yet think about the times in your life that you did not get something or someone you desired. Have there ever been times that not getting things your way has worked out for the best?

Tragically, our culture is filled with examples of people who got exactly what they wanted, and found that it made them very unhappy, or in the worst case scenario, killed them. Michael Jackson will forever be etched in our memories as someone who was able to achieve great levels of fame and fortune through his abundant talent. But ultimately, getting the success he wanted appeared to have played a role in his early death.

We have seen similar scenarios play out in the early losses of Whitney Houston, Heath Ledger, and many other popular entertainers. One could look at the magazines at the supermarket right now, or any entertainment website, and see examples of people who have gotten what they thought they wanted to be happy, only to make unhealthy decisions and become quite miserable.

Most people don't change unless a situation forces them to. They get very comfortable with what they want and then fight change and compromise. Yet more so than any other time in recent history, the economy has forced individuals and families to make great changes in lifestyle choices, living arrangements, and retirement planning.

Every negotiation puts you at an advantage to learn something new, try something different, and gain new insights that you had not learned before.

Those who have weathered the recent recession with the most happiness and serenity have been those who were able to ask, "What is the advantage in this new set of circumstances?" Those who have experienced their recent financial hardships with the most despair and depression have been those who asked, "Why do these bad things keep happening to me?"

If you choose to accentuate the opportunity or "silver lining" inherent in any negotiation process, then you are opening yourself to change, grow, and evolve in ways you never imagined possible. My client Marla articulated this experience after going through a painful divorce, negotiating custody of her eight-year-old son, and then seeing her husband become engaged to another woman:

"In my mind it was like, 'No way am I letting my son near that bitch.' It was bad enough to share joint custody with just him, but now with this new girl, I don't think so! However, instead of automatically assuming that I'm a loser victim who will be lonely while my child is with 'her,' I started to question it. I thought, 'really, what's so bad about her? If she can make my ex happier than I could then say mazel tov to both of them.'

"That's when my son admitted to me that he actually liked this new woman and had been afraid to tell me. He was afraid that I would be too hurt. I realized what my anger was doing to him, to both of us. I also came to see that his visits to his father could be a chance for some 'me' time to be alone in the house, watch what I want to watch on TV, and maybe even to go to some lectures or take some classes. The compromises I made didn't have to be dramatic and awful, they could be advantages for learning and growth."

Creativity: A central theme of Rational Relating is creation; that is, building something that is original, new, and possibly different from what has come before. In order to be truly creative in a relationship, both participants must be able and willing to share and express their own point of view, while opening their minds and hearts to another. Easier said than done!

Think for a moment about a painting that you feel a connection to. What are the colors, textures, and shapes that bring up certain feelings? How did the artist use a blank canvas to bring something to life that had never been seen exactly that way before? And what would have happened if that painter had said, "I think I'm going to try to do this like everyone else"?

Now take a look at your own relationship, either past or present. The moment you meet someone it is a completely blank canvas. There is breadth, there is space, and there is opportunity to paint strokes on an emotional landscape that have never been painted before.

Or, you can fill the space with shapes and figures that try to be like everyone else's. Such a creation may have functional purposes, but it is unlikely to provide a context for creativity, nor lead to a structure that can withstand "little quakes" over time.

In order to strengthen the compromise pillar, each person in a relationship must be willing to engage in the creative process. Therapy can help couples find innovative and inventive ways of negotiating preferences and differences. Using the four previous pillars, couples can learn how to engage creatively by compromising with integrity, strong communication, compassion, and responsibility.

The moment you meet someone it is a completely blank canvas.

Anthony and Michelle used these guidelines to resolve sleep frustrations in their three year marriage. Michelle, a public school teacher, needed seven hours of uninterrupted rest in order to feel at her best during the day, and deal with the trials and tribulations of her students. Anthony had built a very successful plumbing business, which demanded that he work at various hours, and sometimes take emergency calls at night. Both believed it was "normal" for a husband and wife to sleep in the same bed every night.

However, Michelle noticed herself becoming tired and impatient with her students during the day. Furthermore, she was becoming short-tempered and resentful with Anthony over trivial things. At first, she thought these moods may have been linked to job burnout, or even her diet. Then one week Anthony's father suffered a heart attack, and he went upstate to help take care of his family. After that week, Michelle reported feeling more invigorated, awake, alert, and excited about her life than she had in years. Her guilt about feeling so good when Anthony wasn't home was what brought them into couples counseling. "I love him," Michelle shared, "I love our life, I love his body, I love his mind, I love everything about him. So why do I feel so much better when he isn't there?"

This tipped me off that the problem may have been less emotional than physiological. When I asked Michelle what her sleeping patterns were like, she reported that she wakes up several times a night when Anthony is home due to his inconsistent schedule, occasional emergency calls from customers, as well as his snoring and general shifting around in the bed. "But what can I do about that," she asked. "It's not like he's doing any of that intentionally. There's no way to avoid those interruptions and actually get a good night's sleep."

That is where Michelle and millions of couples are wrong. Sleep deprivation and inconsistent rest patterns are dangerous for your emotional and physical health. Recent studies have associated sleep deprivation with depression, poor concentration, hallucinations, aggressiveness, decreases in immune functioning and hormone production, and increases in obesity, diabetes, and cardiovascular disease. In short, consistent sleep deprivation can go a long way toward wrecking one's personal and professional life. Many couples find it challenging to impossible to sleep together. And then we wonder why people feel so "exhausted" all the time?

I helped Michelle and Anthony understand the impacts and side effects of sleep deprivation. Then using Creativity, they began to discuss ideas and solutions that would enable them to feel close, yet still allow Michelle a good's night rest. Anthony did not relish the idea of sleeping without Michelle. But once he grasped the impact of sleep deprivation on her emotional and physical health, he realized it was in everyone's self-interest to compromise.

Eventually they developed a system that allowed them to sleep together on some nights, and have Anthony sleep in the guest room on other nights. Once Michelle started getting more consistent rest, she reported feeling more connected and intimate with Anthony, and less short-tempered and exhausted. Their connection only grew after that, and soon they were able to form creative compromises on their own.

It can be very difficult to actually practice compromise in relationships. It can feel like you are "losing something" when you give up a preference. Even when you see the opportunity to create something new and wonderful, it can be scary. The main ingredient here is willingness to experiment creatively, to "paint" differently, and to experiment with varying solutions.

Humility: Wouldn't it be a great world if everyone just said and did what you think they "should"? Wouldn't life be easier if other humans just agreed to cooperate based on your rules? Wouldn't your life be happier if people would stop disagreeing with you and just do things your way?

The problem is that every other person on earth is walking around thinking the same thing. No two people, even twin siblings, have had the exact same experience. We are all unique individuals who have acquired different hopes, expectations, and preferences in different ways. Therefore it is impossible that there is only one "right" or "correct" way of engaging in relationships.

Humility is the process in which you clearly and authentically are able to say, "Maybe my way isn't always right, but I am willing to learn a different solution." It means giving up attachments and demands that others should do things the way you want them to. And finally, it involves recognizing you are not the ultimate authority on how things should be in your own unique relationships, because there is no final "Truth." You are an active participant in your relationships with others, but you do not have the final say.

This understanding is essential in engaging in satisfying compromise. It allows you to state, "I know my way is not always the right way, so I will create a new solution that involves someone else." Without humility, compromise will look more like, "My way is the right way, but I'll give in on some issues if it means I'll get more of what I want later." This is not true compromise, and ultimately leads to resentments, frustrations, and then damage to the relationship pillars.

"Maybe my way isn't always right, but I am willing to learn a different solution."

Denise and Martin demonstrated the power of humility in a counseling session. They had met at church six months earlier and were beginning to discuss the possibility of marriage. They agreed upon the importance of attending church services and the meaning of religion in their lives. What did they did not agree on was what took place during the social events afterward.

Martin would freely talk to people after services, including single women. Denise, who tended to be more of an introvert anyway, resented Martin's extroversion, became jealous when she saw him talking to women, and fearful that he would leave her for someone else. "When he's with me he shouldn't be talking to others," she said, "His attention should be primarily on me, I'm his woman!"

Martin explained that he had always enjoyed socializing at church events, even before they started dating, and did not want to give that up. Through the process of exploring the "compromise" pillar in therapy, we began to explore the concept of humility. How did Denise know for a fact that Martin "shouldn't" be socializing with others? How did she learn that his talking to other women meant he wasn't interested in her? Why did she think he would drastically change his ways of mixing with others once they became romantically serious?

Through this exploration, Denise conceded that it seemed irrational and unfair for Martin to agree with her on this issue. Nevertheless, she still experienced discomfort and fear when she saw him "workin' the crowd." Through this discussion, and a willingness to engage in creative compromise, Martin agreed to include Denise more frequently in his social activities at church, including introducing her as his primary partner.

Denise liked this, but admitted that she was still very anxious about interacting in large groups the way he did. Martin suggested that when they are in a large room, and he is talking to different people, that he could touch his heart as a demonstration to Denise that she comes first. After trying this out, Denise reported in session, "It worked great. It wasn't exactly what I wanted, but I'm glad I was willing to try to something new. At least the day ended with us feeling close instead of angry."

The Compromise Exercise

In every unique relationship, the issues and struggles are going to be highly specific and personalized. Nevertheless, when taking steps toward creating compromises, I seek to focus on the largest discrepancies that were revealed during Rational Inventory of Values Checklist (from Chapter Four), and then explore where differences lie. The following is a list of the most common differences I have seen in couples.

- sexual frequency
- how money is spent
- how children are disciplined
- where spare time/vacations are spent
- religious / spiritual expression
- monogamy

- location of home / neighborhood
- political affiliation
- involvement with each other's families
- friendships outside the relationship

I then ask each partner to rate on a scale of 1 to 10 how willing they are to compromise on each individual issue. Marking the issue as 1 means the individual is very willing to compromise and try resolving issues in a creative way. Marking the issue as 10 means they are not willing to compromise on a given issue, and these are going to be dealbreakers in the relationship.

Many ask about the appropriateness of holding dealbreakers, i.e., non-negotiable issues. I happen to think that dealbreakers are important when it comes to maintaining one's integrity and compassion. For instance, a dealbreaker for me is physical violence or intentional mental cruelty in a relationship. I won't put up with it in any context, and if I did I would be violating my own standards of integrity and compassion for myself.

Different people have different dealbreakers. Some create dealbreakers around monogamy, religious expression, or any of the ten issues mentioned above. There is nothing inherently "bad" or "wrong" with having clear dealbreakers and strict boundaries.

What *can* be problematic is when someone has an abundance of dealbreakers that prevent the ability to engage in Rational Compromise, and which then prevents them from relating with others. It's one thing to say, "I just can't live with someone who can't manage their finances." It is quite another to say, "I just can't be with someone unless they think like I do, worship the way I do, vote the way I do, live where I live, are the same age as me, the same race as me, and want to home school our children."

The more dealbreakers, the more barriers to engaging in creative satisfying relationships.

What if one person doing this exercise has an abundance of 1's circled, while the other has an abundance of 10's? If one person appears to have a large amount of dealbreakers, and the other appears willing to change and compromise on any issue, then I would go back to the Integrity Pillar from Chapter Four. Is balance a priority in this relationship? Are both expressing themselves in ways that are consistent with their integrity? Does it really make sense for one person to have all the power to make major life choices, or will that imbalance in decision-making ultimately lead to resentment in the long run? A lack of balanced compromises often leads couples to experience distance, anger, and actions outside of integrity.

When It's Over

Not every relationship is meant to last forever. Regardless of what society or religion says about marriage vows and "permanence," it is still a fact that about half of marriages end in divorce, and many non-married couples break up. Sometimes all the compromises in the world don't work. And I don't think that is always a horrible thing.

Relationships can be wonderful conduits for growth, change, love, and expansion. But when a union has become toxic, damaging, stagnated, and destructive, then taking a break can be the most compassionate step you can take for your own well being, as well as your partner's.

The fact is, human beings are constantly changing and evolving every moment. As you read this page, your molecules are shifting, your brain cells are altering, your skin is changing, your hair is growing. When you are mindful of these changes, you can age with improved health, spirit, and vitality. When you ignore or fight these changes you will likely experience struggle, frustration, and oftentimes depression.

Either way, no two people are going to grow and change in the exact same manner. It *is* possible in a Rational Relationship for two people to evolve in a way that is complementary and flexible. When people mindfully act with integrity, effectively communicate, treat each other with compassion, take responsibility, and create compromise, they are much more likely to remain in a loving and supportive union with one another for the long term. But when people grow and change in opposite directions, it can be unreasonable and unfair to require or demand they stay together, or to expect them to compromise on issues outside of their own integrity.

Mary, a 32-year-old newly divorced woman, explained this best:

"My relationship with my husband was so much fun in our twenties. We met in college and loved playing the same sports, going to the same bars, having the same friends, even having the same taste in music. It was so romantic! We got married immediately after school ended, believing that this was going to last forever.

"But things started to change. We both got jobs, had regular work schedules. I still wanted to try new things on the weekends, go to new places, he wanted to stay at home on the couch. He was no longer interested in playing sports, in learning new things, and began drinking more and more beer. Looking back on it, I think he was getting depressed, but he refused to talk about it with me or with anyone else.

"Eventually I realized I didn't need him to go to the movies, to go take a class, to play volleyball on the beach. I started to realize I was having more fun and felt happier without him. That understanding terrified me at first. I talked to him about getting couple counseling so we could communicate more and maybe find some ways to compromise through these differences. At first he agreed to come. But eventually he backed out, saying he didn't think we had any actual problems, that these were "normal" parts of a marriage.

"It hurt both of us when I left. I still have a lot of sadness about this relationship. But I have to tell you honestly, that mixed with the sadness is an incredible sense of relief. I love him in some ways, but I sure don't miss him. He's not a bad person at all. I just want to share my life with someone who can match my energy and interests, and he needs someone more patient and understanding. I'm able and willing to enjoy my life single, and in many ways I feel happier and more alive without him. I definitely believe the divorce was the most compassionate decision for both of us."

How do you know when it's time to call it quits? The key to exploring this question is to use the pillars in this book. There are no hard and fast rules for this. But here are some guidelines to consider:

- If your partner has ever done or said anything to threaten your physical safety.
- If your partner can't or won't communicate about the problems in your relationship.
- If there has been a pattern of lies, deceptions, and violations to the integrity of the relationship.
- If there have been consistent words and actions that lacked compassion.
- If your partner has become uncontrollably self-destructive in a way that compromises your own emotional or spiritual health.
- If you find yourself unable to forgive your partner for a mistake or unwilling to release grievances (see the previous chapter for more about forgiveness).

In a Rational Relationship all stages are infused with integrity, communication, compassion, responsibility, and compromise. It is just as important to remember this at the end of a relationship as it is in the beginning and the middle. This commitment then allows you make decisions with rational clarity and serenity, even when emotionally events are painful.

Biggest Obstacle To Compromise: Fear Of Loss

Let's talk about fear. By now, it wouldn't surprise me to hear you say, "Yes, I have read all this, but in the back of my mind I still have the fear that compromise means giving up something really essential rather than gaining something valuable."

There are many reasons one might react to compromise with a fear of loss. In North American culture, it is often considered weak or submissive to compromise and negotiate. In a society where there is often pressure to be "the best," "number one," or to constantly "come in first," it can be quite scary to admit, "I don't know what is best, maybe I could negotiate on certain issues." Someone who runs a successful company or corporation may find that the resilience and single-minded vision that can build a successful business does not translate well into personal relationships. Indeed it is often those who thrive in business who have the hardest time compromising outside the office.

The biggest misunderstanding around fear is that it is protecting you from something you don't want. Occasionally it can. But when it comes to relationships, fear actually *increases* an outcome you don't want. Snooping is the very best illustration of this principle, as it is a fear based response to abandonment that *only* can result in one person considering leaving the other.

The more dealbreakers you maintain, the more you refuse to compromise, the more you react to fear, the more you will feel separate from others. People who come to me complaining of emptiness, loneliness, and feeling separate from others, generally are experiencing the effects of relating with others from a base of fear. But when you enter into a compromise from the B.E.A.C.H. (balance, experimentation, advantage, creativity, and humility), then you're allowing for joy, play, fun, and fulfillment to prevail.

When it comes to relationships, fear actually *increases* an outcome you don't want.

Bradley and Sara on Compromise

Damon (D): So based on what we have discussed so far, I have seen several issues that are sources of contention. Those are:

- Bradley's preference not to attend Sara's sister's wedding
- Sara's lack of attention to Bradley emotionally and sexually
- Bradley's online relationship with Melissa
- How spare time / vacations are spent
- How money is spent

Are there others I have missed?

Bradley (B): How about the way her family treats me really sucks.

Sara (S): Oh here we go again...

D: I'm going to include that as "involvement with each other's families," to make it more inclusive of future outcomes, fair enough?

B: Fine.

D: So I'm going to ask you now, for each one of these issues, say how willing you are to compromise on a scale of 1 to 10. A 1 indicates you are completely willing to negotiate and compromise on this issue; a 10 is considered to be a nonnegotiable dealbreaker. Remember, this is based on the four pillars we have already covered. You have both expressed consistent integrity, enhanced communication, improved compassion, and increased responsibility in this relationship. Now let's use that to iron out some current and future problems.

[Both Bradley and Sara fill out this sheet, and return it to me with these scores]

	Sara's Rating	Bradley's Rating
Bradley attending Sara's Sister's wedding	5	9
Sara's emotional and sexual attention to Bradley	2	4
Bradley's online relationship with Melissa	10	5
Where to spend spare time and vacations	5	5
How extra money is spent	5	3
Involvement with the other partner's family events	6	8

D: So it appears that when it comes to your sister's wedding, Sara, you have become more willing to compromise, where Bradley is still very unwilling to attend. Fair enough. At the same time, you expressed that Bradley's online relationship with Melissa is not an area you are willing to compromise by rating it a "10," whereas Bradley stated with a "5" that he was open to compromise. So what's the answer here?

S: I will accept you not going to the wedding, I will respect you not going to the wedding. But in return I really want some more quality time alone with you. Without FaceBook, without Melissa.

B: I can totally agree to that. I rated it a "5" because it's not that important. Melissa is an old friend, and yes, it is fun to flirt. But I would rather the time be spent with you.

D: I noticed, Sara, that you marked a "2" on expressing attention to Bradley. Does that mean you are open to compromise?

S: Absolutely. I don't always know what he wants or what he needs. He shuts down a lot, or at least it seems that way to me. He is definitely communicating more now and that helps. I am willing to compromise and try different ways to show him that he does matter to me.

D: And you both expressed feeling fairly neutral about how spare time and money are spent.

B: As long as it is not with her family, I'm very open. I want to please you, Sara. I don't like not giving you what you want, and I know you want me to be able to hang out with your family. That's part of why I always try to buy things for you, to make up for the fact that I can't stand your family and don't want to be around them.

S: And what I want is you. I'm willing to let go of some of the family stuff. I am working on that, I listed it as a "6" here, and that is a result of the compassion we have worked on together. More than having things, I want to be able to feel relaxed with you, laugh with you, see that smile of yours. It doesn't really matter to me where we do that, if it's here or across the world, just so long as we do more of it.

B: Just knowing you want that too helps me feel like I still want to be here, I still want us to work through these issues together. I know I'm not easy to deal with, and I know you've been trying really hard to understand. That means a lot to me.

D: Going forward, there will still be some issues to work through as far as family involvement in day-to-day lives, especially if there are kids involved. But by working so hard together on your relationship pillars, you have shown me and each other how you are able to strengthen the structure of this relationship even when there are outside stressors. The more you continue to reinforce these pillars consistently, the more your relationship will be able to successfully stay solid. It may not always be easy, but you two have proven that it is possible.

Rational Compromise Checklist

The art and skill of compromise is an essential pillar of any Rational Relationship. It involves a strong willingness to be creative and open minded, as well an ability to face feeling fear and loss. Here is a scale of different levels of compromise in a relationship. Where does yours fit?

1. Investments in being "right" without negotiation or interest in bargaining. Consistent use of dealbreakers when differences arise. Both participants may argue consistently and withhold giving in order to prove a point. There may be talk about "revenge" at times and feelings of exasperation.

2. Negotiations from a "win/lose" perspective. Resentments and tensions over past negotiations can be present. Participants keep "scores" or "victories" over the other, and there is a sense of competition in negotiations. However, there is an increased awareness of releasing rigid standards for the greater good of the union.

3. Good ability to flexibly negotiate in some areas, yet hold onto complete rigidity and stagnation in others. There can be progress toward creating a relationship that is balanced, while there remains an abundance of rigid dealbreakers in other areas (example: a couple may be able to decide how to balance a budget, but still argue about where they "should" go to eat).

4. Overall good ability to negotiate problem areas, both partners willing at times to create solutions together, minor investments in being "right," with one or more "third rail" subjects (example: couple can easily negotiate financial or

sexual issues but family-of-origin issues still emotionally charged and tense).

5. Healthy and equitable give and take in negotiations and consistent patterns of creating new paths together that are satisfying and authentically acceptable to both members. Both experience the relationship structure as a "we" versus an "I." There is ease and comfort discussing problematic differences.

CHAPTER NINE

Welcome To Your New Home

Congratulations! You now have all the information to build your relationship "home." A home is a safe place where you can go to relax. It provides a haven and respite from the outside world. It allows you to feel confident, recharged, and able to take on challenges of another day.

If your own relationship is not currently providing this type of sanctuary, then consider what part of the "structure" might need some help. Is it possible that the "House Plan" is off, that your relationship is more about conformity than creativity, or more about grievances than gratitude? Is it possible that your "foundation" is unsteady, meaning that you and your partner are missing the rationality, inquiry, or friendship that provides the fundamental base of a strong relationship home? Or, do one of the "pillars" need reinforcing? Are you and your partner needing to increase a sense of integrity, a process of communication, an expression of compassion, acceptance of responsibility, or engagement in compromise?

None of us is perfect in relationships. We all have good days and bad days. We all have moments when we slide into old familiar patterns; we all have moments that may reflect emotional reacting instead of Rationally Relating.

Similarly, every home has its set of quirks that are unique. Sometimes the hot and cold water are reversed, sometimes there are strange and unusual creaks in the walls, sometimes doors and windows open and close differently in specific weather conditions. Your home is still the place you return to, even with quirks. Just like your relationship can be the safe place to return to even when it's not "perfect." By practicing the same type of upkeep for your relationship as you would your own home, you will increase the opportunities to feel safe, relaxed, and happy.

If your own relationship is not currently providing this type of sanctuary, then consider what part of the "structure" might need some help.

Of course, it is common for any one of us to resist new ideas and creative ways of promoting joy and fun in our everyday lives. When I've shared the ideas of Rational Relating with individuals and couples in my practice, many questions have come up. I hope to address some of these common concerns here. If I have not addressed your question, then please email me at Damon@ DamonLJacobs.com.

"This is all too rational. I'm more of a feeling person." How often do you feel like brushing your teeth? Doing your laundry? Taking out the garbage? Washing the dishes? Saving money? Going to work? Shoveling the snow after a snowstorm?

Taking the kids to their practices / rehearsals / classes? For most, these are mundane and sometimes benign chores that simply get done. It's not as if most people wake up and say, "I can't wait to wash the car today!" But it gets done regardless of how you feel.

Similarly, your day is filled with rational activities that you do regardless of how you feel. If you have access to this book and are able to read it, you must have done something at some point you didn't feel like doing. Going to class, learning to read, studying in school, earning a living, budgeting money, and obeying the law, are not things people feel like doing every day. But through a process of rational (and usually unconscious) thinking, they often get it done.

You may be someone who prefers more heightened emotional states in your primary relationships. You may come from a family where yelling, shouting, crying, and high-stakes drama were the norm. This doesn't mean that you can't choose a more rational path that would allow you to incorporate more experiences of joy, serenity, and calm.

No one is expected to be perfect in this process. This is not an "all or nothing" experience. But in order to create the relationship home you want and deserve, it's going to take some active efforts. Proactively choosing rationality over emotional reactions is the first major step in making this happen. If you can't make that happen, then who can?

"Your stance on monogamy is troubling. Are you really recommending open relationships?" No, I am recommending relationships that prioritize creating over conforming. I support relationships that incorporate authentic communication, consistent integrity, generous compassion, complete responsibility, and active compromise.

If two people use the tools in the "pillars" to create an honest and loving negotiation around sexual and emotional expressions with other people, that is the home that is right for them. If two people use the tools in the "pillars" to create a monogamous structure, that is the right home for them. I have no investment in helping couples practice monogamy or non-monogamy. I do have a passionate interest in helping couples relate to each other with dignity and integrity.

I discussed in Chapter Four "The Myth Of Cheating," i.e., the standards and words couples often use to to position each against the other. In these conversations, there is always a victim and a "bad guy." People take on these dichotomous labels which result in each person feeling disconnected from their partner, and less likely to continue to nurture their relationship structure with integrity. The truth is, most human beings are going to experience a sexual, and sometimes emotional, attraction to more than one person at some point in their lives. Why make something so natural seem so shameful?

I am recommending relationships that prioritize creating over conforming.

Instead of imposing rigid, inflexible, and unrealistic standards that set relationships up for failure, let's get Rational. I work with couples to create conversations about what happens when there are urgings for another, not "if." I help people take preventative measures to maintain their building structures by having rational and compassionate discussions and compromises about monogamy. I facilitate opportunities for partners to share their values, fears, hopes, jealousies, and insecurities in a respectful and compassionate setting. Sometimes these sessions can be very uncomfortable and scary for the participants. But the more they are willing to be honest with integrity now, the less they will need me (or a divorce lawyer) in the future.

"I've tried being rational, I don't seem to be able to do it. I can't get over the pain my partner caused, I can't seem to trust him again." After a violation of integrity, it can be very hard to regain trust. Your partner might be truly regretful and be working hard to be more consistent with his actions. If he expressed himself sexually outside of an agreed negotiation in your relationship, it will be important for him to have a way to demonstrate transparency and integrity that he is not continuing to repeat the same behaviors. That might mean checking in with you at certain times, going to couples counseling, improving his communication, or any number of actions that can rebuild the Integrity Pillar after a major "quake."

However, even in the best of circumstances, you may not be able to quite go back to the level of trust and safety that you felt before. You have permission not to trust him as you did in this past! You cannot go back and undo the wrongs. You cannot pretend you don't know certain things about him. You cannot force yourself to feel something you don't feel.

What you *can* do is shift the focus of your trust back on you. Consistent with the Responsibility Pillar is the assumption that you are one hundred percent responsible for your emotional experience. You can focus on rebuilding the violation of trust you have had with yourself. Did you kinda-sorta know about it beforehand? Are you combing through the details of the past and saying, "I should have known about this"? Are you giving yourself a hard time for turning a semi-conscious blind eye to his indiscretions?

What you *can* do is shift the focus of your trust back on you.

Keep in mind your are not responsible for his actions. But you are responsible for how you *react* to his actions. If you say to yourself, "I did something wrong, there is something messed up about my judgment, I can't ever be happy with anyone, everyone does something to hurt me in my life..." then you will find it nearly impossible to trust anyone in any relationship.

Conversely, try saying, "I may not trust him, but I trust me. I trust my worth, I trust my heart, and I trust that I deserve to love someone who behaves with integrity. Either he will prove he can do that, or he won't. In either case, he is released from being the primary source of my happiness, and I will forgive myself for any way I participated in a violation of integrity that ended up hurting me." Does that feel different?

Is it possible to continue going forward in a Rational Relationship without there being one hundred percent trust? Yes, but it will be challenging for you to be in any kind of relationship if you don't trust yourself. Make *you* the source of your trust, and then you can make clearer decisions about with whom you choose to be intimate and vulnerable.

"I've had an affair, which is a violation of my integrity. Do you recommend I tell my partner?" Not always. I do not subscribe to the idea that every transgression of Integrity has to be shared with one's partner. You can sometimes deeply hurt another person while trying to unload your guilt. When considering telling your partner about any violation of integrity, consider:

1. What is your motivation for sharing? Is it to increase intimacy, or to assuage your guilt?
2. What are the emotional consequences of telling your partner?
3. What are the advantages in sharing? Do the advantages outweigh the potential consequences?
4. Can your partner find out any other way other than from you?
5. Can sharing this information potentially open up new avenues for integrity, communication, compromise, responsibility, and compromise? Can it bring you closer?
6. What would it feel like thirty years from now if your partner still doesn't know?

When it doubt, I recommend working with a Licensed Marriage Family Therapist in your area and sharing the fears/hopes about disclosing violations of integrity in a relationship. When searching, you may want to ask beforehand if they have an all-or-nothing disclosure policy about affairs and secrets, or do they see relationships in more complex shades? Either way, it is vitally important to move forward with Integrity in order not to increase the damage and heartache that violations of Integrity can potentially cause.

"I'm willing to follow the 'blueprint' outlined in Rational Relating, but my wife isn't. How do I make her more Rational and less emotional?" Begin with the Integrity chapter. Use the Relationship Inventory of Values in this book together to see where each of you stands on certain issues. How are her values similar and different to your own?

Then look at the values she lists in her top 10. If she lists "Affection" as a top value, you may say something like, "Yelling at me for not taking out the trash limits my ability to feel open and affectionate with you." If she lists "Tolerance" as a primary value, you may say, "But you are not being very tolerant of me when you scream at me in the mornings." If she lists "Honesty" as a value, you can say, "Then how honest are you being when you say you hate me?"

Hopefully your partner will be willing to read the first few chapters of this book and consider how Rational Relating can make your marriage stronger and more joyful. But even if she refuses, you can still affect the relationship by practicing these tools on your own. Or to put it another way, "Be the change you want to see."

When you live your life with integrity, you encourage others to do the same. When you react and communicate rationally, you set an example others can follow. When you demonstrate compassion and understanding, you increase that potential in others. When you take responsibility for your emotional wellness, you give others permission to do the same. Ideally, it works better when two people in a relationship are mindfully working on their "pillars" together. But it is not necessary to make a relationship work.

"I'm tired of trying. I don't want to be in this relationship anymore. Is that irrational?" Not at all. Sometimes ending a relationship can be the most rational choice you can possibly make. If someone is intentionally hurting you, if they can't/won't act within their Integrity, or if you've simply lost your feelings of love and can't bring them back, then it might be perfectly rational choice to leave this relationship.

Even in this scenario, however, you still have the choice to engage in a process that entails rationality, integrity, and compassion. You have the option to create a sense of closure that will improve the possibility of you being open with another person. You can use a break-up as an opportunity to learn, grow, and evolve in ways that actually assist you in your next relationship.

Sometimes ending a relationship can be the most rational choice you can possibly make.

So often people think a situation has to be really awful to walk away. Your partner has to be "wrong," or you have to be a "victim" in order to say, "enough." However, by perceiving one person as villain, and the other as a hero, you carry these all-or-nothing dynamics into your next relationship, thereby almost guaranteeing the same outcome. This is when you may think, "Why does this always happen to me?" Or, "Why do I always attract the same losers?"

Practicing Rational Relating in all stages of a relationship, including the last one, enables you to form new pathways of emotional connections. It allows you to break toxic cycles that inhibit your ability to make changes in new relationships. It allows you to move forward "unburdened" by emotional weight from your past.

"You seem to ignore gender differences. Isn't that important?" No. There are plenty of self-help books that will tell you that men act one way, and women act another. One very popular book highlights the differences between men and women by speaking as if they are metaphorically from two different planets. The truth is, in nearly two decades of working with couples, I have found that stereotypical gender roles are neither helpful nor accurate.

Are there general patterns? Sometimes. I have worked with couples where the man has difficulty communicating feelings, and where the woman feels rejected by his emotional pulling away. I have worked with couples where the man comes in after having "cheated" and the woman feels mortally "violated" by his poor choices.

But just as often I have listened to women who have violated their integrity in a relationship by sexually acting outside of an agreement, or said or did things to damage the various "pillars." Similarly, I have worked with men who have expressed strong need to experience intimacy, love, and commitment within the context of a monogamous framework. I have seen women withdraw in traditionally "masculine" ways, I have seen men plead for more quality together-time in traditionally "feminine" ways.

When it comes to same-sex relationships, these traditional gender roles are even more obsolete and unnecessary. Contrary to stereotypical notions, same-sex couples do not exclusively take on "male" or "female" roles. I have found that both partners are quite adept at pursuing, distancing, giving, receiving, yelling, crying, loving, and forgiving. There may be general patterns but rarely is there ever strict adherence to simplistic "roles" within the relationship structure of same-sex couples. They are both capable of displaying "masculine" and "feminine" qualities, just like opposite-sex couples.

Furthermore, if a naive therapist *expects* adherence to strict gender roles then they might inadvertently create those imbalanced reactions in the family room. This is why it is particularly important for all counselors to pay attention to their own biases, assumptions, and ways that they are encouraging conformity instead of creativity in their own practice. Without this awareness, therapists and counselors may perpetuate myths about traditional gender roles that serve only to destroy the relationship, not strengthen its pillars.

"This Rational Relating 'home' seems great, but I don't think I can do it." If you can think, you can. If you can talk, you can. If you can use thought to determine some of your reactions, you can. These are basic human skills you need to keep any kind of job or stay out of jail. So if you have ever worked, or spent time outside prison, then you can build your Rational Relationship home.

The question I ask in response is, "Do you *want* a safe and joyful relationship home? Do you *want* to experience the fun and pleasure of engaging in a Rational Relationship? Or do you put limitations on your happiness?"

So many people put an unconscious "glass ceiling" on how happy they will allow themselves to be. They think that a superstitious shoe will drop if they experience too much joy. In fact, it works the opposite.

If you are expecting things to go wrong for you, then you will inadvertently participate in events that go wrong. If you actively seek fault and shame in your partner, you will ultimately find it. If you carry around a belief that you are fundamentally unlovable and undeserving of compassion and kindness, then you will engage in relationships that support that. You will play an active role in your own unhappiness if you sabotage yourself with superstitious notions.

So many people put an unconscious "glass ceiling" on how happy they will allow themselves to be.

Instead of thinking to yourself that you "can't do it," try asking, "How good can I let this get?" Notice your anxiety level subtly creeping up when your relationship is going well. Pay attention to your level of discomfort when you experience joy with your partner. You may experience a gravitational pull toward finding something to worry about during smoother times. Consider working with a therapist on how to expand your capacity for happiness if you are setting limits or boundaries on how good you are allowed to feel.

Relationships don't have to be *that* hard. Now you have the tools to build a beautiful relationship home for yourself and for your partner. It might be a unique structure that is unlike any building that ever came before. Or it might be similar to homes that your parents or friends have. Either way, my hope in writing this book is that you will use these tools to create loving, fun, and meaningful, "homes" with others, and with yourself. Enjoy!

Acknowledgments

A wise woman once said "It Takes A Village," and writing a book is no different. For me it is a joyful yet arduous task that is made possible with support, encouragement, and wisdom from the "Village" of my life. The following individuals, many unknowingly, have played a significant role in bringing this book about.

First I must thank my best friend and "life witness" Matt Cameron for your contributions in my life. Your have been a source of inspiration, education, and strength. There is a part of you in every one of these "pillars," and I am so grateful for your continued encouragement and support.

Jacob Glass has been a never ending source of knowledge, guidance, and humor this past decade of my life. I can only aspire to be as effective in my teaching and speaking as he is in his groundbreaking lectures. Brendon Burchard has generously offered more help and information than I know what to do with to get this book published and to put my career on course. Dr. Debbie Joffe Ellis remains an inspirational and trusted colleague. Her leadership and eloquence in teaching Rational Emotive Behavioral Therapy (REBT) around the world continues to promote global health and healing. Thanks to all three of you for being role models of resilience and leadership.

I am very private with my work before it becomes public, yet there are three therapists I trust whose judgment and input have been invaluable. Gerry Sweetman, Scott Kramer, and Dave Schwing have all guided me personally and professionally during the creation of this book. Anyone in the New York area would be privileged to work with any of them.

Without the support of my brother Jason Jacobs, my life would be very empty. I am constantly grateful and amazed for your presence in my life, Jason, as well as for my surrogate family in New York and California: Michael Santos, Jim Gaylord, Courtney Joseph, Richard Oceguera, Mary Blanchett, Howard Leifman, John Bonelli, Truett L. Vaigneur Jr., Giovanni Vitacolonna, David Derbyshire, Gustavo Monroy, Ryan Lennon, Wendy Brown, Albert Gonzalez, Seema Suturwala, and of course, Nancy "Goldie" Goldberg. I may not get to see you or talk with any of you as much as I'd like, but you have all been an indelible part of my growth as a human being.

I am proud to have been part of the resilient and dedicated staff of Project Achieve, who spend seven days a week working to eradicate the spread of HIV/AIDS on our planet. Thank you to the entire crew for your patience with me while writing this book. In particular, I must offer humble gratitude to Leah Strock, Krista Goodman, Blaz Bush, Travis Cronin, and Michael Henriquez. You all gave me crucial feedback in the early stages of formulating these concepts.

In the last four years I have had the privilege of interviewing over three-hundred actors, writers, producers working in daytime television and in dramatic web series. A few have gone out of their way to offer me guidance, support, advice, and friendship. For this reason I offer a special debt of gratitude to Anthony Anderson, Ian Buchanan, Tom Casiello, Bill and Susan Hayes, Rachael

Hip-Flores, Ilene Kristen, Florencia Lozano, Patsy Pease, Wendy Riche, Tina Sloan, Robin Strasser, Jacklyn Zeman, and Colleen Zenk. You all have inspired me more than you realize.

Working through the editing process with Ed Hayman is always a privilege and a pleasure. Thank you, Ed, for being so very generous and insightful while role modeling such dignity, compassion, and patience.

And finally, there is not enough praise and acknowledgment for the true "pillars" of my life, my parents, Joy and Paul Jacobs. This book is written as a testimonial to your connection, and to your demonstration of what a rational loving relationship can look like for over fifty years. Your support, faith, and encouragement of my work has guided me through every word I've ever written and will always be where I turn for strength and clarity.